QUALITATIVE RESEARCH IN CRIMINOLOGY

Qualitative Research in Criminology

Edited by
FIONA BROOKMAN
LESLEY NOAKS
EMMA WINCUP

Ashgate

Aldershot • Burlington USA • Singapore • Sydney

Published by
Ashgate Publishing Limited
Gower House
Croft Road
Aldershot
Hants GU11 3HR
England

Ashgate Publishing Company
131 Main Street
Burlington, VT 05401-5600 USA

Ashgate website: http://www.ashgate.com

Reprinted 2001

British Library Cataloguing in Publication Data
Qualitative research in criminology. - (Cardiff papers in qualitative research)
   1. Criminology - Research - Methodology
   I. Brookman, Fiona II. Noaks, Lesley III. Wincup, Emma
   364'.072

Library of Congress Control Number: 98-74933

ISBN 1 84014 571 4

Printed and bound in Great Britain by Biddles Limited, Guildford and King's Lynn.

Contents

vi

Acknowledgements

The editors would like to thank all of the contributors to this volume. We extend our particular thanks to Amanda Coffey for encouraging us with the original idea. Our thanks also to the other series editors, Paul Atkinson and Sara Delamont, and to Jackie Swift for her efficiency in producing the text. As editors we have found our involvement with this project both stimulating and enjoyable and it has encouraged us to work together on future research projects.

Introduction

Fiona Brookman, Lesley Noaks and Emma Wincup

This collection of original papers explores the application of qualitative research to a wide range of criminological topics, including traditional areas of criminological enquiry such as violent crime and topics which have only recently entered research agendas, for example, private policing. The publication of this volume in the Cardiff Papers in Qualitative Research series extends an established tradition of qualitative research at Cardiff which has already explored areas as diverse as gender, health and medicine, education and childhood.

Academic scholarship in criminology at Cardiff has a long standing national and international reputation. The high academic standing of the subject area is reflected in a flourishing and vibrant research community involved in both funded research and an extensive range of postgraduate work. Qualitative research methods have served as an integral part of the programme of research undertaken and this text will demonstrate how a variety of such methods can be effectively deployed to extend knowledge and understanding. While this edited collection does not exhaust the diversity of criminological research undertaken at Cardiff, it does give an indication of the range of empirical work that researchers are involved in. All of the contributors are directly linked to Cardiff, either as postgraduates, staff and, in some cases both. All of the chapters discuss research projects which are ongoing or have only been recently completed. In presenting their firsthand research accounts, authors reflexively consider the methodological and ethical questions and dimensions to their work. The volume thus makes a unique contribution to the field of criminology through providing detailed reflexive accounts of the experiences of conducting research. In so doing the book complements other texts on research methods in criminology which primarily deal with methodological issues in the abstract.

Organisation of the book

Chapters in the book are organised around two inter-related themes: the process of criminalisation and responses to crime and criminal activity. In the first section, the concern is with the processes by which certain activities are labelled as criminal and thereby come within the remit of a range of criminal justice agencies. A recurring theme in the contributions in this section is an acknowledgement that the boundaries of criminal behaviour are socially constructed and as such are shifting and fluid entities. The contributions span the historical perspective. Drakeford traces the public order experience of the Greenshirts, a 1930s uniformed political movement which agitated amongst the unemployed and became the only organisation to be prosecuted under the 1936 Public Order Act. Roberts focuses on Speaker's Corner, a public sphere which has its origins in the criminal culture of eighteenth century London. In exploring these diverse research areas, both authors acknowledge that the concepts of crime and deviance, and indeed responses to crime and deviance, are historically relative.

More contemporary activities are analysed in the chapters by Monaghan and Beck. Monaghan's contribution explores bodybuilding as a drug subculture and focuses on this emerging activity located at the boundaries of illegal activity. The links between steroid use by body builders and violence are increasingly made in stereotypical media images leading to moral panics about 'roid rage'. Beck's chapter on indecent exposure addresses a criminal activity which has frequently been represented as marginal and trivial, as reflected in its regular inclusion in so called humorous depictions of the sex offender. The chapters by Brookman and Noaks and Levi focus on different forms of violent crime; homicide and assaults against the police. The area of violent crime is plagued by problems of both under reporting and under recording. Both accounts review the social construction of data concerned with violent crime and consider how qualitative research strategies can go beyond official accounts of the form, content and levels of criminal activity.

The second section of the book is concerned with researching responses to crime and criminal activity. The chapter by Gomez-Cespedes introduces an international dimension focusing on responses to organised crime in Mexico. Such state supported acts are rarely defined as criminal acts despite their illegal status. The chapter provides a detailed account of the process of conducting ethnographic research on this highly sensitive topic and considers the implication of conducting research in difficult social and political contexts. Wincup's chapter also explores her experiences of conducting ethnographic research, in this case, in three hostels for women awaiting trial. She focuses on the appropriateness of feminist methodological approaches when researching women experiencing multiple and complex problems in their lives. Also in this section are two chapters concerned with the occupational cultures of particular criminal justice professions. Cockcroft and Noaks consider the research issues involved in investigating the closed cultures of policing. Both authors make an important contribution to policing research. Cockcroft adds an important historical dimension to existing studies of police culture. Noaks focuses on the emerging private security industry which increasingly 'polices' residential communities. Moving on from a concern with offenders and criminal justice professionals to a concern with victims, Pithouse's chapter deals with the responses to the crime of fraud on the part of victims and explores the generalised impact of their experience of victimisation on levels of trust and confidence in other interactions.

Methodological themes

While all of the chapters deploy some form of qualitative methods, the particular approaches are varied and include interviews, participant observation, focus groups, documentary analysis and oral histories. The contributions show evidence of careful selection by researchers of methodologies appropriate to their research questions. Many of the investigations undertaken are in sensitive areas which have received limited prior attention from researchers and which require a particularly sensitive approach. While such an approach is not exclusively the province of the qualitative researcher, a number of the chapters illustrate the ways in which qualitative methodology is particularly suited to the study of crime and deviance. For example, Pithouse, in his chapter on fraud victims, argues for the appropriateness of a qualitative analysis as the *only* methodology that can grasp the subtle world of social identity, meaning and interaction upon which the crime of fraud is constructed.

A number of the contributors elect to deploy the qualitative method as a means to provide social actors with their own voices. In a number of cases, such strategies provided a unique opportunity for typically silent groups to actively contribute to the research task. Beck, in her chapter concerned with women's experiences of indecent exposure, acknowledges the lack of a victims' perspective in previous work and an overwhelming reliance on offenders' accounts. Her qualitative interviewing and use of focus groups with women allows for a re-evaluation of the crime of indecent exposure which incorporates the views of female victims. Women offenders have also traditionally been an under researched group, particularly when compared with their male counterparts. The development of feminist criminological perspectives has sought to redress this imbalance but inevitably gaps remain in our knowledge of why women offend and how they are treated by the criminal justice system. Wincup's chapter provides an insight into the process of researching the lives of women awaiting trial, a neglected and marginalised group in term of research and policy attention.

A number of chapters draw upon established traditions but focus on new areas of criminological enquiry. Sociological concerns with organised crime have a long history but academic researchers have rarely dared to reveal crimes committed by the state. Gomez-Cespedes' chapter focuses on the ethical issues encountered in researching the politically sensitive topic of organised crime in Mexico. The chapter by Noaks reviews the use of qualitative research methods for researching private security guards operating in a single residential community. While public policing has increasingly come under the ethnographer's gaze, there has been limited attention in the U.K. to the occupational culture of private policing. While the precise subject matter of the chapters in this volume is varied and diverse, many share a common focus on sensitive research topics and all make a convincing case for the value of qualitative methods in furthering the research task.

Although the contributors to this volume all demonstrate a commitment to the value of qualitative approaches, the chapters also contain a critical reflection of the use of different qualitative techniques and discuss potential problems and difficulties. For instance, Monaghan's chapter considers the impact of the ethnographer's perceived status as a group member when accessing the 'closed' world of drug-using bodybuilders. Wincup highlights some of the dilemmas of feminist ethnography, focusing in particular on ethical issues and the emotional consequences of participating in research for both the researcher and research subjects. A number of the contributors also discuss the ways in which their own gender impacted on the research process. Gomez-Cespedes' chapter reflects on how her status as a young Mexican woman directly influenced her negotiations regarding access into official organisations in her home country. Wincup explores the importance of gender in relation to fieldwork in female-dominated institutions.

In addition, several of the chapters in the volume deploy a historical perspective and evaluate qualitative methods pertinent to a retrospective analysis. Drakeford reviews a range of qualitative research strategies, including archival evidence and interviews and debates the ways in which interviews carried out up to sixty years after an event can be used as evidence in social scientific enquiry. Cockcroft's chapter applies a qualitative methodology to the historical dynamics of police culture and provides a review of the effectiveness of the oral history as a means of gathering data. He presents an argument regarding the value of an historical approach as a means of accessing an occupational group with a tradition of resistance and suspicion of external researchers.

A number of the chapters discuss the value of qualitative methods as a means of diversifying a research strategy, typically combining qualitative and quantitative approaches. Brookman's chapter is concerned with patterns and scenarios of homicide across England and Wales and notes the traditional reliance on quantitative analysis in such studies and their shortcomings in capturing the full complexity of the phenomenon. She reviews the value of qualitative analysis of documentary evidence and concludes that some combination of the approaches is the most revealing. Similarly, the chapter by Noaks and Levi argues for going beyond the partial account of police targeted violence that derives from official statistics and quantitative methodologies. In this instance, quantitative crime data were supplemented by qualitative interviews with perpetrators and some analysis of media constructions of the issue. Their chapter discusses the contested meanings that can emerge from such triangulated approaches and the challenges this can afford to officially sanctioned accounts.

In this introductory chapter we have not reiterated each chapter in detail but highlighted the major methodological and analytical themes which feature throughout the text. Our ordering of the themes does not reflect their importance or significance. Inevitably, there will be other themes which occur to readers as they read through the various contributions. The chapters that follow in this volume develop further our initial analysis and demonstrate, in detail, the different experiences of criminological researchers.

Part one:
The process of criminalisation

1 The Public Order Act 1936 and the Greenshirt Movement for Social Credit

Mark Drakeford

Introduction

The Greenshirt Movement for Social Credit - to give its full and official title - is the only example, in twentieth century British history, of a movement made up of members who were regularly in uniform, and suspected of being at the fringes of the law, throughout the interwar period. During that time, the character of the movement altered radically. Its 1930s manifestation as a shirted political movement, marching on the streets, agitating amongst the unemployed in favour of the heretical social credit theories of the Scottish engineer, Major C.H. Douglas[1], had travelled some distance from its 1920s origins as a left-wing, peace-and-woodcraft alternative to mainstream scouting.

The Movement, and its supporters, appear in this edited collection because their activities cast an illuminating light upon two of its central preoccupations: the borderzone between legal and criminalised activity and the dilemmas and potentials which qualitative methods of enquiry provide in its exploration. This chapter focuses upon the response of the Movement to the 1936 Public Order Act and its aftermath. The Act transformed the hitherto entirely legal activity of appearing upon the streets of Britain dressed in the uniform of a political organisation into a criminal offence. In order to make sense of that response, however, it will be necessary to sketch in some brief account of the Movement, its attitude towards acting within and without the law and the response which these activities had already evoked from the authorities.

The account which follows draws upon an extensive archive collected by members of the Movement in the 1970s and 1980s and held at the London School of Economics. It also includes extracts selected from more than twenty in-depth, qualitative interviews carried out over almost twenty five years with surviving members. The nature of this interview material is discussed in more detail later in the chapter. The Archive itself contains

7

material which may be divided into a number of distinct categories. It includes a large number of formal, public documents both produced by the Movement - annual reports, periodicals, newspaper articles and so on - as well as public domain material written about it by others. This category of material intended for public consumption also contains material of a broader nature, dealing with the Movement or its ideas in a wider context. Examples include the dozen or so books written by the Greenshirt founder, John Hargrave, as well as pamphlets and other supportive documents from a range of supporters in the literary world, as diverse as Compton Mackenzie, Ezra Pound and Dorothy L. Sayers! A final set of papers which might be listed under this heading are to be found in collections of ephemera - playbills, notices of public meetings and so on - which, while in full public circulation, were not intended to form any permanent record.

A second category may be defined as material which, while not possessing any claim to confidentiality, was nevertheless not intended directly to be placed in the public domain. Examples include internal memoranda, tickets for meetings to be attended only by members of the Movement, minutes of routine meetings, drafts of documents intended for later publication and so on.

A third category includes documentation which, at the time of its generation, was - implicitly or explicitly - of a private or confidential nature. These include letters between individual members, diaries, minutes of private meetings, correspondence between Hargrave and his leading followers, internal financial assessments and membership records. For the purposes of this chapter, this material also includes the set of documents held at the Public Record Office in London and which includes police and special branch accounts of Movement surveillance which continued throughout its existence.

This chapter aims to make use of information from all these sources. In terms of considering the use of qualitative methods, and in exploring the boundaries of semi-legal and criminal activity, however, it draws most heavily on interview material and upon the contemporary internal and confidential documents in which these questions were discussed and decided upon.

The Greenshirts

The Founder and animating spirit of the Greenshirts was its Leader, John Hargrave. The youngest of Baden-Powell's Scout Commissioners, Hargrave's wartime experience as a stretcher-bearer at Gallipoli had made him resolutely opposed to the semi-military character of the early Scouting movement and the many retired Generals who formed its controlling circles. In 1921, at the home of the Labour activist and leading Suffragette, Emmiline Pethick-Lawrence, he founded the Kindred of the Kibbo Kift, a mixed sex, anti-war youth movement, dedicated to internationalism, an anti-industrial ecologism and - above all - the demand that Youth should supplant the failed policies and personnel which had led the world to the ruin of the Great War.[2]

From the earliest stages, the Movement attracted attention through its deliberate assault upon the conventions of its time. Vera Chapman, an early feminist member, recalled its ethos in this way:

> It was full of exuberance and excitement. It was taken out of this world altogether by a sense of enchantment. You were lifted right out of this world ... It was a magical and religious atmosphere. It was the religion of the spirit which you could not deny, out there under the sky.

Within this atmosphere, the purpose of the Movement appeared to her to be one of,

> peace and better education and the breaking open of various taboos; the taboo against discussing sex, the taboo against throwing off your clothes in camp and the taboo against discussing anyone else's religion. People would be surprised now at what an awful lot of fuss there was at taking off your clothes in camp. People thought us terribly shocking. Well, we broke the taboos against sex, religion and politics which were absolutely sealed down. We broke the seals and brought them into the daylight.

It is not surprising, perhaps, that such flamboyance came to early official notice. Baden-Powell had quite certainly complained to the Home Office about Hargrave - whom he described as 'swollen-headed and communistic' - at the time of the Kibbo Kift's foundation. He hinted darkly to any Scouts who were thinking of following Hargrave into the KK that the Movement and its leaders were under the official surveillance of the security services. In fact, the Public Record Office at Kew holds a large Kibbo Kift file containing reports of Home Office and Special Branch interest in its affairs throughout the interwar period and beyond. An early example, dated 23rd May 1925, arose from a complaint made by an employee at the Central

9

Office of the Conservative and Unionist Party who complained that the Kibbo Kift was part of an expanding youth movement conspiracy to undermine the social order, full of 'singularly repulsive types', much given to 'the singing of German songs - (and of English ones as an afterthought)'. The Special Branch Report prepared for the Metropolitan Police made it clear that, 'we watched the Kibbo Kift very closely', before concluding that, 'any undue publicity would only help the organisation to expand'.

Indeed, while the Kibbo Kift continued to attract public and more covert attention throughout the 1920s, it was not until the conversion of the movement into its Greenshirt phase in the first half of the next decade that its relationship with the forces of law and order became problematic. The activities of the Movement were essentially street-based, involving large-scale street corner meetings, sale of the Greenshirt newspaper, *Attack!*, and participation in unemployed worker demonstrations and rallies.

While it is not part of this chapter's purpose to discuss the scale and scope of the Movement, its membership, at its height, was numbered in thousands, rather than hundreds. Members were concentrated in London and the industrial North of England, but contained members and branches as far apart as Cardiff, Glasgow, Belgium and Brisbane. In the public discussion of the Public Order Bill, for example, it was cited by the daily *Reynolds News* as, 'by far the most numerous wearers of political uniforms in this country' (25.2.34.). In its one foray into electoral politics, at South Leeds in the General Election of 1935, it outperformed any other Shirted and any non-parliamentary party during the whole of the inter war years. In the twenty days of campaigning 3642 electors had been persuaded to vote for the Greenshirt candidate, representing 11.01 per cent of the votes cast.

Hargrave always stressed publicly that the Movement should operate entirely within the law and that disciplined conduct would, by itself, separate the Greenshirts in the public mind from its more notorious rivals, the fascist Blackshirts and the red-shirted brigades of the Independent Labour Party. The stance was pragmatic as well as principled, however. Despite their ambitions to recruit amongst the unemployed, the core Greenshirt leadership continued to be drawn from the peace-activists of the Kibbo Kift days. While members were, almost by definition, prepared to behave in ways which drew attention to themselves, they remained essentially mild-mannered and anxious about their reputation. When members carried out a carefully planned demonstration at a Test Match, for example, they waited until the lunch interval so as not to cause any inconvenience to other spectators!

Nevertheless, as the climate of physical antagonism between the shirted movements deepened in the mid 1930s, the level of planned and unplanned violence was also on the increase, especially at street level. The atmosphere of competition and its potential outcome were described by as respectable a figure as Andrew Carden - a Greenshirt and public school man who was later to become a distinguished architect - in this way:

> The Fascists and the Communists were trying to hold meetings in the East End, with quite a lot of threatening stuff there. We used to go down there in groups and stand behind the fencing and the results were quite satisfactory. It was intimidation of a sort. I broke a Fascist's jaw once, although that was by accident. They never succeeded in breaking us up on the streets although down in Clerkenwell and one or two places like that they tried a bit of it.

The Public Order Act 1936

The Greenshirts were first discussed in the House of Commons, in a public order context, when the Labour M.P. for Durham, Mr Leslie, asked the Home Secretary, 'whether in view of the recent raid by a body of Fascists upon the rooms of the Social Credit Party at Liverpool, and the attack upon three lads - two of whom had to be removed to hospital - and in view of other acts of violence by Fascists, he would consider the suppression of the Fascist organisation'. Sir John Simon replied, noting that four people had been committed for trial as a result of the attack and preferring to wait for the outcome before taking any further action (New Age 4.6.36.).

At the end of August 1936 widespread publicity, in newspapers and on radio, was given to an attack on a body of uniformed Greenshirts who had taken up position at the head of an Ex-serviceman's Demonstration Against Fascism in central London. Similar reports were forthcoming from other parts of London and the North of England. During the early autumn, the Government intention to introduce a Bill prohibiting political uniforms was widely canvassed. By October, when it was clear that action was to follow, the Greenshirts began to prepare their defence. On the 10th October, the General Secretary, Frank Griffiths, issued a Press Release which contained the essential argument upon which the Movement was to rely in its protest against the Bill:-

> It is a mistake to suggest that the wearing of ALL political uniforms is provocative. On the contrary, as the police are well aware and the press have often reported, the uniform of the

Greenshirts provokes applause everywhere. In fact, it has become the symbol of discipline and good order throughout Great Britain.

The Public Order Bill was published on Armistice Day, November 1936. The threat of violence and intimidation from the Fascist Blackshirts of Sir Oswald Mosley lay behind the Bill, although there were those in the wider social credit movement who thought that Hargrave's wilder calls had brought their own reward - 'JOIN IN THIS STRUGGLE FOR LIFE OR GET SWEPT OUT OF THE WAY BY 'THE MOB'! - AND TO HELL WITH YOU..DOWN WITH THE BANKERS COMBINE AND (YES!) DEATH TO THE BANK OF ENGLAND' (Broadsheet 115, January 1936). His immediate reaction to publication, however, was to issue a statement that while, 'I do not support the authorities wish to hit at an organisation like ours, which has a very good record for orderliness and good discipline', nevertheless, 'as ours is a political organisation, we shall comply with the law' (Youth Archive: 56). The press release was widely carried in newspapers and formed the basis of the Movement's main attempt to influence the legislation.

Once the Bill came before Parliament a large scale lobbying operation was mounted. A special issue of *Attack!* was published in which the Green Shirt use of the uniform was defended in terms, once again, of the asset it provided for the maintenance of order, as well as putting the civil liberties case for the uniform as the 'poor people's poster'. *Attack!* was sent to every member of the House of Commons and to supporters in the Lords. Ninety visits were made by Greenshirts in uniform to Parliament during November, with between 30 and 40 uniformed men and women present on all occasions while the Bill was debated. Individual Greenshirts pressed particularly for the placing of an amendment which the Movement had professionally drafted, limiting the ban on uniforms to their use in public meetings. Attempts were made to influence the debate by using contacts with M.P.s who had previously been sympathetic.

These efforts produced almost the only notes of dissent which were raised during the swift and unamended passage of the Bill through Parliament. During its Second Reading on 16th November an attempt was made to restrict the provisions to the Blackshirts. Sir John Simon, for the Government, disagreed: 'I hope the House will take the view that we should prohibit the wearing in public of political uniforms as right. This does not apply merely to the Fascists...Some people may think that nobody else is trying to wear a political uniform. That is not so. Apart altogether from the Greenshirts, information is coming in of other people, largely of

12

the anti-Fascist persuasion ..... adopting the wearing of uniforms.' The Green Shirt defence, taken up by a number of M.P.s on their behalf, was that their use of uniforms was not in itself a threat to anyone. The Liberal M.P. Kingsley Griffiths differed from the Home Secretary: 'I am very sorry at the moment for the poor old Greenshirts, if I may call them that. They are a perfectly law-abiding body of men, and have never done anyone any harm... Their activities will be curtailed by the operation of this Bill, which they did nothing to provoke.' These efforts, combining the contributions of individual Liberal, Labour and Conservative M.P.s, continued right to the end of the parliamentary process. They were unsuccessful, but remained the only serious and sustained attempt to alter the Government's proposals.

By the end of November the Bill was law. It was not to be enacted until 1st January 1937 and, for a short period, the Movement looked for ways of circumventing its effects. Polly Bush, diminutive ballet dancer and childhood member of the Kibbo Kift, later to be arrested for calling 'Social Credit is Coming' from the public gallery of the House of Commons, recalled her Greenshirt attempts to prevent Police intervention in continuing meetings:

> I did a great deal of chatting up the police around the corner while they got down to business. I really did. I used to get someone to buy some Mintoes. If you've made sure they've travelled in somebody's back pocket and got them a bit hot and tacky before you start giving them away, by the time the policeman had unravelled them, or I'd done it for him if the weather was cold and he had his gloves on, popped it in his mouth, which included standing on tip toe. By the time he got himself nicely gummed up it was too late to shout for help!

The Act and its aftermath

Soon, however, the impact of the Public Order Act upon the Greenshirts was to be profound. It deprived the Movement of its most potent form of advertisement and undermined the value of those public activities which it continued to undertake. These consequences were quickly apparent in the context of the Public Order Act itself. In the middle of 1937 the Attorney General launched two prosecutions against individual Greenshirts who had conducted public meetings in Luton and Camberwell. On Saturday April 24th 1937, 34 men and women members of the Party visited Luton Permission had been secured in advance from the Police for the holding of

13

a public meeting. They used equipment designed to draw attention to their presence - drums, flags and torches. Many but not all were wearing some of the green buttonhole badges, arm badges, ties and other emblems which members had been urged to take up once uniforms themselves were banned. The group had marched through the town arriving for a meeting at Market Hill at about 8.10 p.m. The routine order of such a meeting was carried out. Torches were lit, songs were sung and the speakers delivered their message. Permission was sought of the police officer present to march back to the outskirts of the town, and this permission was granted.

At the end of the meeting the names and addresses of three speakers were taken and the Chief Constable reported proceedings to the Attorney General. A decision was made to prosecute the speakers under the Public Order Act on the grounds that the combined effect of equipment, insignia and green items of clothing amounted to a uniform, under the meaning of the Act. The case was heard before Magistrates in the town. The defendants' solicitor told the Court that it was only the second case heard anywhere under the Act. The case was dismissed.

In Camberwell Magistrates Court, however, shortly afterwards, a case was brought against Green Shirt Douglas Wright who was said to have addressed a meeting in uniform at Camberwell on 27th April. This time the prosecution case had been prepared more carefully. Two officers of the Special Branch were called to give evidence. Detective Sergeant Jones had called at the Social Credit Party Headquarters in plain clothes and purchased material to prove that the organisation was a political one. Detective Inspector Whitely was called as someone who, 'during the course of your duty, attended meetings, marches and demonstrations organised by the Social Credit Party'. He gave evidence as to the nature of the uniform. The bulk of the information was given by uniformed officer P. C. Diamond who referred to the 'Social Credit Party or Greenshirts, as they are commonly called'. He had, he said, 'a good working knowledge of the uniform of the Party' as 'I have attended hundreds of their meetings'.

The case was proved. In the words of the presiding Magistrate:

> The defendant was dressed as described by the officers in a public place - in fact he was addressing public meeting. Was he wearing a uniform signifying his association with this Party, of which it is not disputed he was a member? In my view, he was...Here is a speaker; he gets on the platform, takes off his coat and there he is with a green armlet and this tie, which, of course, can only properly be worn by the members of this

Party. I think these three things constitute a uniform signifying his association with the Party.

The individual was released under the Probation of First Offenders Act - one of the least serious courses of action open to the Court but one which placed a restraint upon future behaviour of a similar kind. The Party did not possess sufficient money to launch an appeal and the conviction remained one of only a handful ever prosecuted under the Act. For the Greenshirts, however, it meant the end of the phoney war. There were to be no further attempts to stretch the meaning of the Act. Instructions were issued through the Broadsheet to avoid any suggestion of uniform, through the wearing of green sweaters or insignia. Even the carrying of green umbrellas was to be forsworn.

'Under normal conditions', said Alex Townsend, 'maybe the banning of uniforms would not have affected the Greenshirts. But these were not normal times.' While street activities continued right through 1937 and beyond, the spark had gone. Recruitment to the Movement had more or less ended. Those who came to new prominence in the last few years of the 1930s were already members, whose enthusiasm and temperament could be turned to the new temper of the times.

In doing so, the Movement relied more upon the willingness of such individuals to engage in actions which were directly against this law. This represented a significant shift in the intentional practice of the Movement. It had long found itself on the fringes of the law and, in the case of the Public Order Act, had seen some of its core activities redefined as criminal. Now, for the first time, it knowingly and deliberately set out to seek publicity for its cause by engaging in acts which were unambiguously unlawful. Categories of crime are, of course, socially constructed, moveable and open to competing redefinitions. Muncie 1996: 13ff), for example, explores the notion of crime as 'historical invention', in which shifting patterns of power and politics combine to 'supply to some people both the means *and the authority* to criminalise the behaviour of others.' Even those without such power, however, have the capacity to shape their activities along the shifting boundary of legality and criminality. As far as the Greenshirts were concerned, the wearing of uniforms for political purposes during the first half of the 1930s had been unambiguously legal. The planned ambush of Prime Minister Stanley Baldwin during the General Election Campaign of 1935, was less straightforwardly so. Here, a group of Greenshirt supporters, learning that Baldwin was to come to Leeds, where the Movement had put up a social credit candidate, hid on the Prime Ministerial train, claiming to a be travelling rugby team. They emerged from the train, however, in full Greenshirt uniform, and surrounded Mr Baldwin at Leeds railway station in a scrum which required the intervention of large numbers of police officers, rather than a referee. No arrests, but substantial publicity followed. Once the uniformed days were over, however, the Movement depended for public attention upon more clearly illegal acts, such as that carried out by Ralph Green, the Greenshirt who shot an arrow through the window of 10 Downing Street on the eve of being called-up on 1st March 1940. The incident made headlines over three days in the British press and radio, with extensive coverage in Australia, Canada and the U.S.A.

A more sustained campaigner was a relatively new recruit, Herbert Gaskoin Cornish-Bowden, to give him the full name by which he was always identified in Special Branch Reports. The son of a Colonel, he had himself been educated at Wellington and Sandhurst before it became as clear to the authorities as to himself that he was not suited to a life of regimentation. The Green Shirt movement gave him plenty of scope for freer expression. On October 11th 1937 'HANDS OFF ALBERTA![3] appeared in green paint 18 inches deep on the wall of the Bank of England: 'his visits to the Bank of England were usually to help decorate the outside of it' remembered Andrew Carden. He had been put up to it by another militant member, Wilfred Price - 'I put the idea to Cornish-Bowden who at the time was unemployed. He was arrested and the Magistrates had him put down for medical attention as a way of smearing him d'you see.' When he appeared again a week later his solicitor, Mr Kennedy - who was to represent both the Movement and individuals within it during their increasing clashes with the law - explained that his client 'held somewhat advanced political views, but he now realised that he went the wrong way to work in order to air them' (The Times 6.11.37). In fact, the seven days spent in Brixton jail were not the last which Cornish-Bowden was to spend in prison for Green Shirt activity. He was in further trouble with the Police in 1939 for aiding and abetting another Green Shirt in causing an obstruction and for fighting at a Fascist meeting, an incident which is best recounted in his own later recollection:

> The average man is a coward, really, isn't he and I don't suppose I am any different. I was involved in a fight once, at a Mosely meeting. We were carrying a banner and a chap tried to pull it down. I gave him a biff. I found myself on the floor with about four people kicking me. Unfortunately, it was very dark and when one is lying in the gutter being kicked it is rather difficult to distinguish one person's legs from another. And I

caught hold of a policeman's foot. Got hold of his toe in one hand and his heel in another and twisted it. Of course he fell down. Next thing I knew either three or four policemen were carrying me out of the meeting, one on each arm like that with one or two holding my feet. What they call the frog-march. They fined me £3 at the London Magistrates Court. That was the only fight I was ever really in for social credit.

Now, a week after Ralph Green's arrow-shooting, he hired a taxi and threw a life-sized effigy of Montague Norman onto the steps of the Bank of England, as the taxi slowed down outside. The effigy bore the slogan 'End Hitlerism. Social Credit is coming'.

The Police went to considerable lengths to secure a conviction. The taxi driver was traced and called to give evidence at the Mansion House Justice Room on 2nd April. The case was widely reported in the papers. The Daily Telegraph on 3rd April informed its readers that: 'A life-sized effigy of Mr Montague Norman, who was yesterday re-elected Governor of the Bank of England, was produced at the Mansion House yesterday, when it was stated that the figure had been seen to roll down the steps of the Bank's main entrance'.

Cornish-Bowden was sentenced to three months imprisonment with three months hard labour. The incident shocked the Movement. The harshness of the sentence and the apparent lack of justice were recalled vividly by members more than forty years later. Wilfred Price vigorously attacked a system which allowed the Lord Mayor of London to adjudicate in cases which involved a protest against City institutions. For Polly Bush, characteristically, it was the human dilemma which was most vividly recalled: 'I went to see him in prison, going as the 'prisoner's friend' because I wasn't a relation. It must have been agony for him being in there. I know it was a political thing - he hadn't murdered anyone, but the incarceration was frightful'.

The incident remains a vivid reminder of the human costs which individuals were prepared to bear in pursuit of their commitment. 'He was a magnificent man' said Andrew Carden, 'and he took action which caused him real agony'.

This chapter now turns to consider the issues which arise for the researcher when attempting to organise and analyse material of this scale, nature and provenance. Methodological questions in relation to qualitative evidence, in particular, will form the focus of the section which now follows.

Questions of methodology

What are the methodological issues which arise from this account of Greenshirt activity and, in particular, from the negotiation of the borderzone between legal and criminal activity with which it has been concerned? Much of its factual content has been put together from a variety of sources, including the public and private written records of the Movement and the accounts of its activities to be found in the newspapers and journals of the time. Insight into motivation and action, however, comes from the more detailed qualitative interviews, some of which have been drawn upon in this chapter. These interviews were conducted between 1976 and 1993. The selection of interviewees was determined by a series of factors, largely outside the control of the researcher. The most significant included longevity - not all members had survived the thirty five years or more since the Movement ended - and accessibility. The decision of some prominent former members to establish an Archive of Movement material provided the catalyst for bringing together individuals who had been out of touch with one another since before 1939. Contact with surviving members proceeded largely by piecing together a series of individual networks, in which one person provided the address of, or revived the interest of, another. To a significant extent, of course, such a process of selection is a random one. It depends upon chance connections and is biased towards those whose interest in the Movement was significant enough to turn any chance connections into renewed contact. Undoubtedly, the individuals available for interview excluded the large number of short-term and peripheral members who flooded in and out of the Greenshirts at the peak of their success in the mid 1930s. Yet, examples have been quoted in this chapter of individuals who were involved from the earliest days - Vera Chapman - and those who joined only towards its close - Cornish Bowden; it has included members who were clearly in the 'officer' class - Alex Townsend - and those, such as Wilfred Price, who were socially and practically amongst the rank-and-file. While gaps and biases remain, the material available is more striking for its variety and representativeness, than its uniformity or partiality.

If obtaining access to interview subjects raises methodological as well as practical questions, the analysis of interview content is even more formidably problematic. The reliability of memory and the weight which might be placed upon recollection has to be considered, particularly when, as in the case of the material included here, such material is drawn from individuals up to sixty years after events had taken place, and up to eighty years since individuals interviewed had first become members of the Movement. Available evidence (see, for example, Bahrick, 1975 and 1984;

18

Parkin 1993; Conway and Rubin 1993) suggests, in fact, that ability to recall information deteriorates very slowly. Cross-checking with contemporary sources suggests that, in practice, interviews with surviving Greenshirts found a high degree of reliability of factual material provided by interviewees.

The ability of older respondents to provide an accurate recollection of names, dates, locations and so on is not, however, either the greatest source of controversy in the field, or the primary concern of this chapter. Rather, discussion has focused around the way in which, 'memory is much more than recall of past stimuli. It involves emotion, will and creativity in the reconstruction of the past to serve present needs' (Coleman, 1986: 2). The view of memory as reconstruction rather than reproduction (see, for example, Gittins 1979, Lieberman and Tobin 1983, Coleman 1986, Rubin 1986, Andrews 1993 and Collins et al 1993) contains within it a series of practical and methodological questions which impinge upon the extent to which this sense of reconstruction can be authentically achieved. These include the quality of interaction in interviewing (see, for example, Cottle 1982 and Marshall, 1986), the communication of mutual interest in the subject under discussion (see Thompson 1978) and the achievement of rapport (see Cornwall and Gearing 1989).

The accounts contained within this chapter are best regarded as the product of individuals attempting to make sense of their own histories and to do so in the context of the changes which have gone on around them. Reconstruction of this sort, however, provides a number of further methodological questions which are particularly important in relation to recollection of actions which lie at the borderline of criminality. The issue of power relations between interviewer and interviewee in qualitative research, especially, lies very close to the surface of such encounters (see, for example, Wilkinson 1986 and Harding 1987 for a feminist commentary on these questions; Briggs 1986 and Bhavnani 1990 address the same issues more generally).

In most considerations of this area writers note the extent to which power rests in the hands of researchers, rather than research subjects. Andrews, for example, (1993:57) notes, 'Not only is the relationship between researcher and researched inherently unequal, but... there is potential for this imbalance to be compounded'. While not seeking to deny the strength of these observations, it is important to note the ways in which - particularly in relation to contentious or difficult material - power imbalances are also capable of being resisted or redressed. The power to withhold information, as well as to seek it, is not always sufficiently understood or valued. Interviewees are not the helpless players in the dialogue which some analysts imply (see Hammersley and Atkinson 1995 for an endorsement of this suggestion). They retain, and use, certain important advantages, of which the power to decide how much or how little to say remains the most essential.

In the case of the Greenshirts, the potential sensitivity of these issues was exacerbated by a series of conflicting considerations. For some - like Andrew Carden or Alex Townsend - respectable careers, both at the time and subsequently, made too direct an admitted involvement in borderline-illegal activity threatening to other important part of their lives. For others - like Vera Chapman, married to a Devon clergyman - there were considerations beyond work to be weighed up. Those involved in an undeniable way in criminal trouble - such as Cornish-Bowden - worked hard to smooth out any impact which their participation might have had in later life, as his opening remarks when interviewed illustrate. Living at this time in the small Devon village of North Bovey, a Union Jack was fluttering from a flagpole alongside the road to guide visitors to the house: 'because they can't call me a Bolshevik if I put the flag up a few times each year, on the Queen's Birthday and so forth. And anyway, what's wrong with the flag of our country as an ornament?'

This chapter ends with a more detailed analysis of one account of a particular incident in Greenshirt history, attempting to draw out some of the methodological issues which it raises for qualitative inquiry.

The passing of the Public Order Act had the effect of turning Greenshirt activity to more directly illegal paths. One direction in which this proceeded concerned a deepening schism between the Hargrave side of the social credit movement and the far-less militant followers of Major Douglas himself. Matters came to a head in May 1938 at a meeting called by the Douglas wing, to hear a report from G.F. Powell, an emissary whom Douglas had sent to Alberta, on his return to London.

The account which follows was provided by Wilfred Price, interviewed at his home in Hebdon Bridge in Yorkshire, more than forty years after it had taken place. Price was a militant member of the movement and a convinced social creditor who continued, at the time of interview, to be an active agitator on its behalf. Within the Greenshirts, despite his intense commitment, he remained a rank and file member, never enjoying for example, the social and personal relationship with John Hargrave which was characteristic of the Leader's contact with many others of his devotees. His recollection of the Chiltern Court meeting ran as follows:

Well, by that time we had a belly-full of the Secretariat. Hargrave was particularly bitter ...and we decided the night

20

before to go and bust this meeting up. Well at any rate we went there. Of course, in those days, it was after the Public Order Act we were not in uniform. We went in plain clothes and the moment Powell started speaking we just started to shout him down and then some of our chaps went on the platform and virtually shoved him off and then started addressing the meeting and then pandemonium broke out all over the place. Then Hargrave entered *in uniform*, stood on a table, made a declaration and then disappeared Then Douglas come in shortly afterwards and the meeting decided to sit down and have its refreshments. So having been in disorder it calmed itself down and started discussing various things.

In the general disorder, however, the police had been called. An Inspector, three sergeants and thirty constables arrived, with the support of a police van. By this time, Green Shirt 'shocktroopers' were in control of the meeting, having occupied the platform and appointed a Chairman. Hargrave had disappeared as dramatically and rowdily as he had arrived. The police made no arrests but remained in the hall during dinner, in order to prevent further disorder from breaking out (Youth Archive: 45).

The Chiltern Court meeting is the single most dramatic episode in which Greenshirts acted on the basis of physical force and with deliberate menace. Hargrave's uniformed appearance and demagogic performance left even his closest supporters with a feeling of ambivalence. 'In retrospect I think it was a mistake' said Wilfred Price, 'I think we shouldn't have done it, certainly not the way we did'.

The account set out above makes it clear that the Chiltern Court events fell directly within the category of planned and intentional illegal activity, to which the Greenshirts had increasingly resorted after the 1936 Public Order Act. An Inspector, three sergeants and as many as thirty uniformed police officers suggest that the level of lawbreaking was not trivial. Price's account has to be explored against that background. It presents an immediate problem of disclosure and characterisation. The speaker begins by suggesting that the incident was premeditated and planned - 'we *decided* the night before to go and bust this meeting up' - before drawing back from such a direct admission - 'well at any rate we went there'. Deniability, even at the distance of nearly half a century, retains an influence over the account we are offered. As well as direct presentation of motivation, the account communicates an ambivalence through its *tonal colour*. The predominant tone is one of scandal and excitement, with the regret at its demagoguery beginning as an undertow and ending as the ascendant emotional colour.

Methodologically, some of these difficulties are more easily solved than others. The questions of fact - was the incident preplanned? has the speaker exaggerated or mistaken the scale of the trouble? - are most easily resolved. Triangulation, through the accounts of other interviewees and through written evidence in contemporary journals and other sources, allows for the details of Price's account to be established or contradicted. In fact, and in line with the findings of earlier investigators cited earlier, the factual content of the spontaneous memory recorded displays a high degree of accuracy, both in general and in detail.

Far more problematic are questions of interpretation. Methodological progress now depends not simply upon the text itself, or its factual corroboration, but upon an ability to contextualise the particular account within broader knowledge of the speaker and the part which the recorded incident may have played in her or his wider relationships and progress. At the heart of the ambiguity which Wilfred Price displays lies two competing loyalties. John Hargrave's appearance in this account may be that of *deus ex machina* but a *deus* none-the-less. Loyalty to the memory of the charismatic leader jostles here, however, with a greater loyalty to social credit itself. At a lower key, loyalties to the place of the Greenshirts within the social credit movement and to certain standards of conduct - it was Price who staged the lunch time invasion of the Test match - also compete for precedence. Methodological understanding of events which cross the border of acceptable conduct require an understanding of motivation as well as action and insight into motivation depends upon those qualities of empathy and rapport discussed above.

At the basis of interpretation has to lie some understanding of the different strands which are present within the messages which this account attempts to convey. As suggested earlier in this chapter, accounts of past events involves reconstruction as well as recollection on the part of the interviewee. In this example, Wilfred Price may be seen struggling to make sense of, as well as remember, the night at Chiltern Court. Given his core commitment to the radical wing of the movement, he retains a clear impression of the incident as a victory for the Greenshirts over the Douglasites. Given his longer-term, and still-surviving, commitment to social credit, he reconfigures his recollection to emphasise those elements which were most distasteful to him at the time and which contributed, with hindsight, to the declining force of the movement as a whole. Of course, these interpretations draw upon a further layer of reconstruction involved in the analysis of such interview material. Not only is the interviewee reconstructing past events in the light of subsequent knowledge and experience, but the researcher is engaged in reconstruction at a number of different levels. The interview itself is a process of drawing from the interviewee an account of events and opinions which places a shape upon that material for which the interview itself provides a framework. Analysis of results involves an interpretation of what is said which draws upon a range of documentary material and, perhaps more significantly, the information and interpretation provided by other interviewees. A series of judgements, then, are involved in which these different layers of reconstruction are laid upon one another.

Conclusion

In summary, then, this chapter has attempted to debate the ways in which interviews carried out up to sixty years following events can be used as evidence in sociological and criminological inquiry. It has done so within the particular context, and the enduring dilemmas, which are posed by the interface between ideological dissent and illegal activity for those whose personal and political lives are otherwise law-abiding. The negotiation of the borderzone between legal and criminal activity provided a tightrope along which the Greenshirt movement had to make a continuously negotiated progress. Understanding that progress demands an attentive, informed and critical qualitative approach. Methodologically, attentiveness is required to catch and reflect the particular voice of the individual, attempting to grapple with the complexities and contradictions which such dilemmas pose. That voice has then to be understood through a method which is informed by a knowledge of the wider contexts - social, historical and relational - within which sense can be made of individual accounts. A critical application of both attentiveness and understanding results in that series of caveats and questions which this chapter has attempted to raise concerning the nature of knowledge, interpretation and reconstruction which are inherent to the qualitative inquiry. When these qualities can be brought together, then it provides a method through which the issues and dilemmas which surround as sensitive an area as changing definitions of criminality and legality can be illuminated and better understood.

Notes

1. Major Douglas had 'discovered' social credit in the years immediately after the First World War. Social Credit was heretical in the sense that, almost twenty years before Keynes' *General Theory*, it suggested that the problem of an industrial economy was essentially underconsumption, rather than overproduction. In order to overcome this difficulty, Douglas suggested that the connection between income and employment should be broken. A 'National Dividend' should be issued to every citizen, as of right, which would be sufficient to support a reasonable lifestyle without the need to compete for scarce employment. The Greenshirt campaign was chiefly founded on the demand to Issue the Dividend, while Keynes, on the first page of his seminal *General Theory of Interest and Money* included the following citation: 'The idea that we can safely neglect the aggregate demand function is fundamental to Ricardian economics, which underlie what we have been taught for more than a century...The great puzzle of Effective Demand... could only live on furtively, below the surface, in the underworlds of Karl Marx, Silvio Gessell or Major Douglas!'

2. Hargrave's influence, as a Youth Movement figure, was substantial. Although outside the scope of this chapter, useful accounts of his conspicuous influence upon the German Wandervoegel and other continental movements can be found in Lacquer (1961). In Britain, the flourishing Woodcraft Folk, are direct descendants of the Kibbo Kift, having originally formed the Co-operative element within the Kindred (see, for example, Paul 1929; 1977 or Springhall, 1977).

3. The only Social Credit government in the world had been elected, in July 1935 in the Canadian prairie province of Alberta. The provincial government's attempts to introduce legislation in relation to the issue and cancellation of credit were progressively frustrated by the federal authorities acting - as all true social creditors believed - under the instructions of the Bankers.

References

Andrews, M. (1993) *Lifetimes of Commitment: Ageing, Politics, Psychology*, Cambridge: Cambridge University Press.

Bahrick, H.P. (1984) 'Semantic memory in permastore: Fifty years of memory for Spanish learned in school', *Journal of Experimental Psychology*, 113:1-35.

Bahrick, H.P., Bahrick, P.O. and Wittlinger, R.P. (1975) 'Fifty years of memory for names and faces', *Journal of Experimental Psychology*, 104: 54-75.

Bhavani, K.K. (1990) 'What's Power Got to Do With It?: Empowerment and Social Research', in Parker, I. and Shotter, J. (eds) *Deconstructing Social Psychology*, London: Routledge.

Briggs, C. (1986) *Learning How to Ask: A Socioloinguistic Appraisal of the Role of the Interview in Social Science Research*, Cambridge: Cambridge University Press.

Coleman, P.G. (1986) *Ageing and Reminiscence Process*, London: John Wiley.

Collins, A.F., Gathercole, S.E., Conway, M.A. and Morris, P.E. (1993) *Theories of Memory*, Hove: Lawrence Eelbaum Associates.

Conway, M.A. and Rubin D.C. (1993) 'The Structure of Autobiographical Memory', 103-137. In Collins et al. (1993) *Theories of Memory*, Lawrence Eelbaum Associates, Hove.

Cornwell, J. and Gearing, B. (1989) 'Biographical interviews with older people', *Oral History*, 17: 36-43.

Cottle, T.J. (1982) 'The Life Study: On Mutual Recognition and Subjective Inquiry', in Burgess, T.G. (ed) (1982) *Field Research: A Sourcebook and Field Manual*, London: Allen and Unwin.

Gittens, D. (1979) 'Oral History, Reliability and Recollection', 82 - 99. In Moss, L. and Goldstein, H. (eds) (1979) *The Recall Method in Social Surveys*, London: University of London Institute of Education.

Hammersley, M. and Atkinson, P. (1995) *Ethnography: principles in practice* (2nd edition), London: Routledge.

Harding, S. (ed) (1987) *Feminism and Methodology*. Milton Keynes: Open University.

Laqueur, W. Z. (1962) *Young Germany: A History of the German Youth Movement*, London: Routledge & Kegan Paul.

Lieberman, A.M. and Tobin, B. (1983) *The Experience of Old Age, Stress, Coping and Survival*, New York: Basic Books.

Marshall, J. (1986) 'Exploring the Experiences of Women Mangers: Towards Rigour in Qualitative Method', in Wilkinson, S. (ed) (1986) *Feminist Social Psychology: Developing Theory and Practice*, Buckingham: Open University Press.

Muncie, J. (1996) 'The Construction and Deconstruction of Crime', in Muncie, J. and McLaughlin, E., *The Problem of Crime*, London: Sage, 5-64.

Parkin, A.J. (1992) *Memory, Phenomena, Experiment and Theory*, Oxford: Blackwell.

Paul, L. (1929) *The Folk Trail*, London: Noel Douglas.

Paul. L. (1977) *First Love*, London: SPCK.

Rubin, D.C. (ed) (1986) *Autobiographical Memory*, Cambridge: Cambridge University Press.

Springhall, J. (1977) *Youth, Empire and Society: British youth movements, 1883 - 1940*, London: Croom Helm.

Thompson, P. (1978) *The Voice of the Past*, Oxford: Oxford University Press.

Wilkinson, S. (ed) (1986) *Feminist Social Psychology: Developing Theory and Practice:* Milton Keynes: Open University Press.

Youth Archive: *The Kibbo Kift Youth Archive*, London School of Economics.

2 Investigating a 'criminal' public sphere: reflexivity, law and class struggle

John Michael Roberts

Introduction

In our 'post-/late-modern' times, the concept of 'reflexivity' has gained increasing purchase within social science. For those using qualitative research methods in criminology, especially the research method of ethnography, reflexivity is often seen as the basis from which the researcher can assess their impact upon the research setting and vice versa. However, although many criminological studies utilise this concept, it is sometimes difficult to know exactly where to locate the 'reflexive Self'. For example, should we restrict reflexivity to those relationships which we directly observe and participate? If we do take this option then we risk by-passing the impact of social structures which we can never directly observe. The fact that many of those who do espouse reflexivity tend to be transfixed by a dualism which posits unobservable entities as external, static and secondary to the lived experience of the researched need not also bind us to that dualism. By focusing upon a public sphere, namely Speakers' Corner, I will argue that it is indeed crucial for the reflexive enterprise to take account of unobservable mechanisms, particularly law and the state.

Speakers' Corner is a particularly interesting empirical site because the twin issues of free speech and public order inhabit its very foundations. Indeed Speakers' Corner currently resides in a space once occupied by the most famous place for public executions in eighteenth-century London, namely Tyburn hanging tree. It will be an integral part of my argument to suggest that the criminal culture surrounding Tyburn historically structured Speakers' Corner and thereby constituted the fundamental mechanisms which endow Speakers' Corner with its peculiar characteristics. Consequently Tyburn's scaffold culture contributes to the social processes which structure the frames of meaning of both researcher and researched. I will base my argument on recent advances in realist and Marxist social theories.

27

Reflexivity and the problem with ethnography

Speakers' Corner

In the north-eastern corner of Hyde Park a strange phenomenon transpires on 'God's day of rest'. Once you realise that this phenomenon is nothing other than speaking you might relax. After all, is speaking not the very essence of our social life? If social life is characterised by clichés, I would reply that appearances can be very deceptive. This corner may very well be characterised by speaking, but it is also much more than this. It is not only that people speak, it is how they speak, what they speak about, the interventions by hecklers, the interventions by audience members, the alliances formed, the strategies pursued and the smashing of common sense beliefs. In other words this corner is a highly structured and complex social context, or public sphere, for people to engage in debate and discussion.

Part of its complexity relates to the official recognition of public speaking in Hyde Park. Principally a series of political demonstrations in Hyde Park erupted at a specific juncture in British history when the question of democratic inclusion in the political process was increasingly going beyond its liberal confines. Major disturbances had been recorded in Hyde Park over the issue of the franchise, the most serious being the 1866 Hyde Park riot which had precipitated after a meeting organised by the Reform League. Following this major disturbance Parliament frequently debated the right to free speech at Hyde Park (Belchem, 1996; Finn, 1993; Harrison, 1965). In 1872 the government passed *The Royal Parks and Gardens Regulation Act*. Among other things the 1872 Act demarcated a space within Hyde Park where people could engage in public debate and discussion. The 1872 Act also laid down a set of guidelines which ensured that certain utterances, such as blasphemy and swearing, would not be heard (Coleman, 1997, pp.31-39; Huggon 1977, pp. 3-13).

Speakers' Corner is an interesting site to research. Hundreds still turn up every Sunday to debate and discuss a whole range of public issues. I spent nine months observing and participating in these issues during 1996. I also devoted a substantial amount of time exploring the genesis of Speakers' Corner through archival data and through secondary information written by social historians. During my 'ethnographic experience', I became particularly interested in the 'inclusive' nature of Speakers' Corner. By 'inclusive' I mean that Speakers' Corner empowers voices which might remain silent in more conventional social contexts. Discussion varies and ranges from utterances by orthodox Islamic speakers to those by gay and lesbian speakers. Common sense ideas, my own included, are regularly

28

attacked in the process. Let me explain the consequences of this for ethnography.

Constructing reflexivity

The most basic assumption underpinning ethnography suggests that in order to understand a specific social context you must actually have 'been there' and observed, perhaps participated, in the social activity which constitutes the context in question. Once returned from the field, you must think about your research material by 'being here', back in your own lived context. 'Being an ethnographer is to be in two places at the same time' (Pearson, 1993, p.ix). Part of the reason for 'being there' in the first place is to gain empathy and understanding (*verstehen*) of the participants involved, 'trying to think oneself into the situations of the people one is interested in' (Armstrong, 1993, p.5). This particular ethnography rests upon the assertion that although there are 'facts' out there, these are only true within the social context of their discovery and only within their textual representation (Van Maanen, 1995, pp.22-23).

An integral part of the ethnographic process is reflexivity. According to Steiner (1991), reflexivity in research practice denotes the turning back of one's experience upon oneself. Caught up in this act is a recognition of the socially constructed nature of both the research self and research experience.

> We are talking about a circular process, in which reflexivity is the guiding relationship allowing for the circularity. This looping back may...unfold as a spiralling, if we allow for multiple perspectives, and acknowledge that 'the same self' may be different as a result of its own self-pointing.
>
> (Steiner, 1991, p.21)

Reflexivity refers to the ability of the researcher to tell a story about their Self so that they become aware of their own research activities. Escaping from the subject-object divide which has so haunted social science implies recognising the negotiated nature of both researcher, research context and the researched. Only then will meaningful dialogue between all three develop. Thus ethnography, according to Clifford Geertz, should strive for 'thick description'. Ethnography's import, on this understanding, lies in discovering 'a stratified hierarchy of meaningful structures' by which certain social acts are important to the people carrying out those acts (Geertz, 1993, p.5). So that the researcher can reflect upon the social context in question; to move 'from local truths to general visions' (p.21). The ethnographic procedure itself must be separated from the interpretative, theoretical moment.

Reflexive struggle

Speakers' Corner undoubtedly represents a rich web of signification. But Speakers' Corner is more than this. As I mingle with the regulars, as I partake in the activities of Speakers' Corner, as I heckle, debate, discuss, listen, and speak, I find that I am actively constructing the social context of Speakers' Corner. My intervention in all of these practices significantly shape the particular social encounter I observe. Even if I watch 'silently' my very presence within a social encounter can provide an input. A speaker might address me and use me as bait in their dialogue. Or I might be 'pulled' into a discussion and asked my opinion on a particular subject. Many regulars often use me as a 'sounding board' to talk about other regulars for whatever reason. My conscious and unconscious intervention in these various social encounters reproduce the wider social context called Speakers' Corner.

Gradually I have come to realise that my very presence contributes to the structuring of the form and content of the social encounters I witness. But I also now realise something else. Structuring is not only a one-way process. Within the boundaries of Speakers' Corner I am not only 'a researcher'. Various encounters 'position' me as heckler, speaker, regular, researcher, non-Muslim, Westerner, European, discussant, sinner, socialist, liberal, white, heterosexual. Even so, as much as these identities are fluid, they only gain a particular credence within the specific context of Speakers' Corner. It is not simply the case that I am viewed as a 'European'. It is also the case that being viewed as a European within Speakers' Corner implies that my biography as a white person can be publicly questioned and reinterpreted. Speakers' Corner thereby encourages an 'inversion' process to occur in the sense that marginalised groups can attack symbols of their oppression. This inversion process is itself encapsulated within the generic and stylistic forms of speaking, discussing and debating; peculiar only to Speakers' Corner.

Here we come to the root of the problem. Some ethnographers, those who are usually labelled as 'social constructionists', stress intentionality at the expense of social structures, conceiving the latter as no more than an external constraint. My experience is different. Speakers' Corner is a recognisable social structure enshrined in legislation. At the same time it is a social structure which sparkles. Speakers' Corner is a moment of wider,

30

conflictual and antagonistic social relations in the sense that it is historically, socially, economically, politically and ideologically structured. Speakers' Corner is therefore a social structure with intentional and meaningful social behaviour residing within its very foundations. But how do we unite structure and agency in a theoretically coherent manner which can be significant for social research? Let us return to the notion of reflexivity.

Towards a materialist theory of reflexivity

If I actively contribute to the structuring of Speakers' Corner, in whatever measure, then it makes no real sense to locate myself as external to the activities which I encounter. I must take seriously the saying that 'honesty is the best policy' by being open about my presence in the research context. This involves suppressing a contemplative stance. Kevin Dwyer (1982) suggests three steps to achieve this 'suppression'. The first step is to see the encounter between myself and the researched as being 'sequential'. It occurs over time. Dialogue within this sequencing is recursive to the extent that it depends upon previous meanings constructed in the encounter. Secondly, each encounter is contingent. Just because I made successful contact with some participants, I could not presume that this would always be the case. Finally, each dialogic encounter is socially mediated through the social context of Speakers' Corner; a context which transcends participants even if those participants also reproduce that context (Dwyer, 1982 p.274). If dialogue between the researcher and the researched is highly structured in the manner argued by Dwyer, then the most suitable way to proceed may not be to simply focus on ordinary everyday practices. A better starting point might be one which began from a high level of abstraction.

Abstraction seeks to discover the necessary properties and relationships of the person, context or object in question. Among other things, abstraction puts to one side contingent and external relationships and properties in order to concentrate upon essential and internal characteristics which shape the research context. These internal characteristics help us to understand the 'causal powers' and 'generative mechanisms' which imbue a research context with particular relationships. Causality, as used here, alludes not to a relationship between discrete events, namely the empiricist definition of causality (A causes B), but rather alludes to what a context or person is like, namely the 'power to' act in a certain way irrespective of whether the context or person will act in that manner within a contingent

31

situation (the internal structure of A irrespective of its contact with B) (Benton, 1981; Collier, 1994; Sayer, 1992).

This theoretical standpoint implies that we postulate a rich or 'deep' ontology which recognises the complex and stratified nature of the world. We can say that a world exists both independently of our knowledge (the intransitive dimension) while also recognising that access to that world is achieved through knowledge (the transitive dimension). Properties, relationships, causal powers, or whatever, may never be observed directly, though we can gain adequate knowledge of them through our practice (Bhaskar, 1978). People, in their day to day relationships, therefore possess 'causal' powers which exist at different levels of society and which are bound up with social structures operating independently of their knowledge. Nonetheless the interaction between these different levels empower agents with capabilities and resources so that they have the 'power to' act in specific contexts and thereby gain knowledge of those structures.

This realist position feeds into the remarks on reflexivity in three ways. First, it suggests that as a researcher I am caught up in relationships existing within the intransitive realm of which I possess no knowledge. Secondly, however, it also suggests that I gain adequate knowledge of this intransitive realm from the standpoint I choose to adopt. Standpoint refers to the site consciously occupied by the researcher in order to produce knowledge in a theoretical and practical manner (Cain, 1990, p.132). Thirdly, two reflexive levels can be noted: (a) *personal reflexivity* in which I present descriptions of my changing relationship with those whom I research (the social constructionist model); (b) *theoretical reflexivity* in which I identify my standpoint and think about the production of knowledge which emerges therein (the realist model) (Cain, 1990, pp.132-3; see also Cain, 1986; Kerruish, 1990).

Yet a problem remains. We are still none the wiser about the specific dynamism which propels Speakers' Corner to reproduce itself and its contradictions, if any. Nor do we know much about how Speakers' Corner has evolved from one epoch to another, or evolved periodically within an epoch. Neither do we know much about why others may view that transition and evolvement through an alternative framework (see Weeks, 1981, p.11; 1997, p.91). The difficulty with the realist definition of reflexivity therefore lies in a failure to understand theory as reflecting upon and inhering within a practical, historical and contradictory world. That is to say, realist scholars still tend to distance the theoretical moment of research from the practical moment because concepts and categories employed are ready-made and simply imposed upon distinct ideological forms of human activity. To overcome this difficulty we need to engage in another reflexive level which can be termed *practical reflexivity*. This is a type of reflexivity in which the 'theorisation of its object, of its presence within its object and the validity of its categories (as categories appropriate to the theorisation of precisely that object) are not three conceptual moves but a single totalisation' (Gunn, 1989, p.93).

Although practical reflexivity is clearly materialist in its outlook, in the sense that theory and practice are distinct reflections of an objective world, it is not at all apparent how we are to achieve such a 'totalisation'. Advice from Karl Marx can be of some assistance here. He encourages us in *Das Kapital* (Volume 3) to seek out how

> the specific economic form, in which unpaid surplus-labour is pumped out of direct producers, determines the relationship of rulers to ruled, as it grows out of production itself and, in turn, reacts upon it as a determining element. Upon this, however, is founded the entire formation of the economic community which grows out of production relations themselves, thereby simultaneously its specific political form
>
> (Marx, 1966, p.791).

Speakers' Corner represents a distinct moment in this contradictory relationship between rulers and ruled. Thus Speakers' Corner assumes a specific ideological and contradictory form in the reproduction of those social relations. By mapping out this form the possibility arises of investigating it historically, tracking down its changing ideology, and investigating the relationship between generic activities (e.g. speaking and heckling) located therein. Ideology, on this estimation, can exist in two guises. 'Critical' or 'negative' ideology is a set of ideas endeavouring to mask and distort class contradictions at the level of knowledge. 'Neutral' ideology is a set of ideas attached to different individuals or social groups. Although such ideas may contribute to domination they do not entail an epistemological distortion of a contradictory reality (Larrain, 1994). There is a dialectical interplay of both forms at work in each social form and, as we shall see, at play in Speakers' Corner.

By taking history seriously in this 'objective' sense, namely the examination of distinct forms of existence related to a mode of production, I arrive at another reflexive level which can be termed *historical reflexivity*. Its advantages are five-fold. First I retain the benefits of the realist position, namely the positing of a rich ontology, but go beyond inherent problems associated with realism, namely its lack of specificity. Secondly a number of ideologies are comprehensible which exist only within our social relations and only within a certain form such as Speakers' Corner. Thirdly I occupy a standpoint which is inherently critical of my own cultural world and of the methods used to elicit information, for it seeks to observe from the historical limits of our social relations (see Lemaire, 1991). As such I avoid being drawn wholly into the hermeneutic world of the participants observed. In effect I occupy two standpoints: one which examines the lived world of the researched and another which endeavours to connect up those beliefs to specific social relations. The first standpoint propels me to be a 'concrete insider' while the second propels me to be an 'abstract critical outsider' (Mattick, Jr., 1986). Fourthly historical reflexivity avoids a symbolic and textual reading of the research context because it grounds research practices within the production and maintenance of the context in question. Immediately, therefore, I begin to ask how meaning is constituted, maintained, distributed and controlled. I simultaneously concretise the production of my own research techniques by saying something about the historical and political context through which I gain knowledge (Scholte, 1986, pp.10-11). Consequently, and finally, I cannot merely read day-to-day activity off from one privileged 'base', such as the economic base. Instead historical reflexivity maintains that I must understand the qualitative characteristics of a social form.

If Speakers' Corner legally sanctions the 'right' to free speech in a public park then the foregoing remarks imply that the form which law and social rights assume under capitalism must be outlined *before* I examine the relationship between those rights and Hyde Park. I start with the first requirement.

The right to free speech and the form of law

How should we view rights within our specific social relations? On a general level, and noting that Speakers' Corner arose through class struggle, we can begin by accepting the advice from Chamblis by conceiving lawmaking as a process seeking to resolve historically grounded contradictions, conflicts and dilemmas arising from class relations (Chamblis, 1993, p.3). This being the case the examination of the right to free speech must eschew any attempt to simply regard this valuable democratic ideal as a legal entity (Kairys, 1982). That is, rights enjoy both legal and social status, the latter extending beyond jurisprudence to encompass political aims and strategies (Gramsci, 1986, pp.246-253; Hunt, 1981a, p.16; On the notion of 'social rights' see Freeman, 1982; Fudge and

Glasbeek, 1992; Herman, 1993; Hunt, 1990). On this understanding the idea that law and rights are mere instruments of a ruling class is untenable. Such a view cannot understand why each assume specific forms in the first place, nor understand how each are distinct moments in contradictory social relations (Pashukanis, 1983; cf. Balbus, 1977).

Consequently, I will offer a brief sketch of the form of law and of rights, in order to gain a set of theoretical tools which are (1) specific to our social relations, whilst (2) enabling us to chart the emergence of Speakers' Corner through those social relations. This sketch will thereby allow us to (3) map the ideological form of Speakers' Corner at a high level of abstraction so that (4) we arrive at a base from which we can say why others might view the same reality through an alternative framework. Finally (5) my approach will license us to occupy two standpoints simultaneously so that a contradiction between belief and action by participants can be discerned.

At an abstract level, namely at the level of commodity relations, we discover two individuals who face one another in an antagonistic relationship. Each wishes to assert their right to claim property. The most basic level at which right exists is with the total social experience of capitalism. At this level we arrive at the peculiar, 'double-nature' of right. Right is expressed in the property and its protection of and by another. This is decisive, as Kay and Mott observe, on two fronts:

> first, in deconstructing property by showing that although it is apparently sustained by a reprocity of interests, it is actually rooted in force and violence; and second, in showing that force in political society is not a phenomenon *sui generis* but an aspect of property and contract
> (Kay and Mott, 1982, p.61; see also Kay and Mott, 1984; Kay, 1988).[1]

Under this definition the atomised legal subject of liberal theory, a subject who interacts on equal terms with other subjects through the market place, is simply false because 'right to' is both the private property of one person as well as being the private property of an Other. It is the private property of an Other because only through the 'right to' property can meaningful exchange exist (see Beirne and Sharlet 1982, pp.318-320; Collins 1982, pp.108-11; Fine 1979, p.43; Picciotto 1979, p.170; Warrington 1981, p.11; Urry 1981, pp.109-110).

With the increasing separation of the labourer from the means of production and the emergence of wage-labour, 'right' is subsumed under specific class relations and integrated into the claim of 'freedom'. The labourer now has the right to sell labour power to whoever they wish and has the right to be free from the ownership of production (Marx 1988; cf. Clarke 1991). But beneath this right lurks the right of capital to exploit labour by extracting surplus-value. More importantly, right now assumes an 'abstract' form which is no longer the property of any one individual. As an abstract and independent form, right is given content and enforced through the public body of the state. The state enshrines the universal form of right (Kay, 1988, pp.122-3).

The capitalist form of the state therefore lies in its separation from the means of production and the power at its disposal to impose the power of money and the rule of law upon civil society, these being the appearance of capitalist social relations to the state (Clarke, 1988, pp.120-151; see also Corrigan and Sayer, 1981). Through recourse to legal precedent the state must endeavour to regulate alternative and distinct claims of 'right' as they appear in different social forms. Within the material body of the state, law achieves this by recognising every person as a subject of right. Law attempts to close down alternative renderings of 'right' as they open up within social forms by placing subjects in particular legal positions such as that pertaining to citizenship. Law maintains a 'disciplinary network' by producing a 'background ideology-effect' within the material body of the state and acts as a 'second-order' discourse for a diverse range of discourses. These can then be invoked when primary discourses are challenged. In order to accomplish this task, legal discourse must perform as the main discourse of closure, consistency and calculability (Woodiwiss, 1985, 1990, 1992; cf. Hunt, 1985, pp.30-31; Kay, 1988, pp.127-128; Poulantzas, 1978, pp.76-92; Santos, 1985; Sumner, 1979, p.246 ff.).

The task now at hand is to inquire into the constitution of the right to speak at Speakers' Corner, how this right is filtered through a number of levels and how this filtering influences my research project. Moreover, this will allow me to explore Speakers' Corner as an historical and social entity, existing in its own right, as well as developing a notion of reflexivity specific to, and historically structured by, Speakers' Corner.

Scaffold culture and the constitution of Speakers' Corner

Clearly the most probable starting point when examining the constitution of Speakers' Corner would be to investigate the 1872 *Royal Parks and Gardens Regulation Act*. On reflection, however, this seems highly unsatisfactory. For Hyde Park was established as a political meeting point decades before 1872 even if its status as a space for public discussion had not been legally recognised. For the 1872 Act regulated the political claims of subjects. As such the transpositioning effects of law can only be assessed at a low level of abstraction because the claims are not, as yet, related to the totality of capitalist relations. Indeed, the most that the 1872 Act can tell us is how individuals, affiliated to certain political groups, socially constructed their aims and strategies. We learn very little, however, about the ideological form of those aims and strategies. For example, it is not at all clear on what basis we can survey the contradictions between belief and action of the groups campaigning for free speech in Hyde Park. From which social class did they emerge? Did they claim universal rights? Or did their belief in free speech at Hyde Park serve to exclude others, such as unskilled workers, from democratic process? We must conclude that the 1872 Act certainly codified and regulated Speakers' Corner but did not constitute it.

Therefore the transpositioning effects of law at Speakers' Corner must be located elsewhere. I believe that the historical structuring of Speakers' Corner lies with the most famous place for public execution in England during the eighteenth century, namely Tyburn hanging tree. Located at the intersection of Oxford Street and Park Lane, a stones throw away from the north-east corner of Hyde Park, Tyburn represents a changing form of English law in the eighteenth century. With the growing discipline of the 'abstract' capitalist market came an increasing propensity for penal law to assume the form of rationality, individuality, and the protection of both property and the 'public' good. A growing belief amongst the elite stressed the realignment of sovereignty to punishment together with a close association with money (Thompson, 1980, p.87). These changing sentiments were reflected at Tyburn. As Linebaugh suggests, a clear relationship at Tyburn in the eighteenth century can be discerned between property and punishment when we consider its quantitative relationship to money. For example, goods stolen which had a monetary evaluative worth of 10d meant a whipping. Those of 4s. 10d merited a branded hand whilst those of £10 or over signalled a hanging (Linebaugh, 1991, pp.80-82).

If, as Douglas Hay suggests, the hanged body at Tyburn became a symbolic recognition of the class struggle and as it dangled on the rope it unleashed defiance and disrespect for the law and scorn for justice (Hay, 1975, p.55), then Tyburn represents the constitution of Speakers' Corner for a number of reasons. First, this criminal public sphere demonstrates the class character of Speakers' Corner in its most basic form. That is, the transpositioning effects of law seek to reinforce the rights and duties of the fundamental signs of capitalism, namely law and money. Class struggle at Tyburn therefore revolved around abstract property rights. This meant that scaffold culture resonated a proletarian moral economy by establishing a genre of marginalised or subaltern dialogue concerning law and exploitation. Indeed many prisoners played to and interacted with the crowd and conducted parodic dialogue and discussion with it (Gatrell, 1994, pp.32-33), while friends and families retrieved the hanged body from the clutches of the authorities, so saving it from being sold for dissection and so preventing it from being turned into a commodity (Linebaugh, 1975; Richardson, 1989).

Scaffold culture thereby transgressed the limits of the exclusionary confines of rational-critical discussion, discussion predicated upon property rights, and so transgressed the limits of the ideological form of the bourgeois public sphere.[2] Scaffold culture demarcated a proletarian public sphere not because those waiting to be 'launched into eternity' came from an emerging working class. Rather those who were to swing at Tyburn attacked the very foundations and ideology of rational-critical discussion by illustrating the bourgeois form through which such discussion was filtered. Scaffold culture illustrated this exclusionary form by refusing to separate law from exploitation. Scaffold culture was an inclusive form of discussion because it was not based upon access to property. The supposed universality of rational-critical discussion was rejected by relating such discussion to its inherent partial and exclusionary form.

Back to the ethnographic experience[3]

If I wish to utilise and develop this initial exploration of the form of Speakers' Corner, the following recommendations provide a useful starting point. They also provide a summary of what has been argued so far.

Ontological recommendations

Ontological recommendations include the following: (a) tracing the historically structured nature of the social context under consideration in order to tease out its specific social characteristics as they relate to the strategic manoeuvres of wider social relations, especially to regulatory bodies (see Jessop, 1990). In the case of Speakers' Corner, I must explore how its form as a context which transgresses the limits of abstract, rational-critical discussion changes through time; (b) exploring different generic forms of activity along with their causal powers (e.g. the genres of speaking and heckling in the case of Speakers' Corner); (c) stressing the necessity of theory in order to search for historical structures not immediately apparent to the naked eye and to think about the emergent properties and experiences emanating from those structures; (d) maintaining a link to the empirical world which facilitates both a point of entry and exit to the 'unobservable'. Thus we cannot deal only in theory but must ensure that theory has a reference point in the 'everyday'; (e) finally, if we wish to include the 'everyday' in our analysis we must have a hermeneutic dimension to our investigation. In many ways this can be accommodated by taking account of genres because genres enable people to discuss matters within a specific form (see Medvedev, 1978).

Methodological recommendations

Methodological recommendations include the following: (a) a move from the most abstract and simple characteristics of the form in question to its concrete and complex manifestations; (b) the retroaction of concepts and categories. Retroaction delineates the requirement to trace the inner and developmental tendencies which exist between forms of existence, forms which are peculiar to capitalist social relations. Thus concepts are validated 'by the argument as it unfolds, by its ability to explain the developmental tendencies of capitalism, and by its ability to account for the phenomena that apparently contradict the validity of the initial categories' (Postone, 1996, p.141). Moreover by placing social theory within the very dynamic of social relations, we develop categories which are not only historically specific but also highlight the possible historical negation of those social relations; (c) historical research, such as archival research, need not be undertaken in a linear fashion such as the accumulation of 'factual stories'. Historical inquiry, by tracking down inner connections between research material, must instead be seen to differ from the mode of presentation of research material. The former seeks out 'tendencies' while the latter presents those tendencies in actual historical development (Marx, 1988, p.102).

Epistemological recommendations

Epistemological recommendations include the following: (a) drawing out different ideological strands in order to analyse the relationship between critical ideology and neutral ideology within a distinct social form; (b) stressing that our knowledge as researchers is produced from a standpoint and is therefore ideologically loaded; (c) underlining also the belief that knowledge can be produced which inheres within the lived world of the researched whilst standing outside of that world at the same time. The latter

39

views the first from an inherently critical position because its categories are constructed from a standpoint that wishes to negate our social relations (see above); (d) the emphasis upon the historically structured nature of the context in question implies that relationships undergo constant change. Research must have sense of duration to the extent that it seeks to understand those changes over time (Cain, 1990, p. 138); (e) ethically, therefore, we must be open to the encounters we witness and admit our influence. At the same time this admits to our practical relationship to the world and establishes a dialectical relationship to our theory.

Conclusion

The intention behind the argument presented was to provide a basis for discussion of the use of ethnographic approaches to explore criminological topics. The overriding concern of the chapter has been to highlight some of the dangers and pitfalls involved in basing one's analysis upon the lived context of the researched. Such an approach, while containing obvious benefits, is more often interested in the social construction of particular contexts rather than social structures existing independently of agents. In this respect some ethnographers actually start their respective social investigation with the same set of theoretical assumptions held by empiricists. Both share the belief that appearances are the essence of social knowledge. As such both, in their own way, deny the causal efficacy of a stratified reality upon people, a reality not immediately penetrable to the naked eye.

I have also been at pains to argue that it is not enough merely to include social structures within the research process. Highlighting structures as well as agency usually results in presenting theoretical recommendations so general as to deny the specificity of distinctive social relations. Therefore I suggest that structures should be analysed within the dense network of distinctive social relations so that the particular structure under investigation can be seen as a qualitative moment of those social relations. More to the point, I believe that history should not be read in a linear manner but should be read dialectically. This is neither to deny the distinctiveness of the social context in question nor the distinctiveness of different epochs. It is to suggest however that both carry with them a permanence; a permanence which resides in the contradictory foundations of capitalist production (Clarke, 1992, p.149). Specificity is the key to success.

Notes

I would like to thank Fiona Brookman, Lesley Noaks and Emma Wincup for their incisive comments. All errors are of course mine.

1.	Contract law is thereby the most ideological aspect of law 'for the practical meaning of the market system was that people conceived of as interchangeable productive units ('equality') had unfettered mobility ('freedom') in the market' (Gabel and Feinman, 1982, p.176).

2.	According to Habermas (1989), 'rational-critical discussion' was predicated upon access to information, the pursuit for a set of general norms and the existence of equal status between discussants. However this was a one-sided description of the public sphere, as Habermas recognised, because it only explored the social characteristics of the *bourgeois* public sphere. For a variety of different perspectives on this subject-matter see Craig Calhoun (ed) *Habermas and the Public Sphere* (1996).

3.	The form and content for this section owes a great deal to Cain (1990, pp. 137-138).

References

Armstrong, G. (1993) 'Like that Desmond Morris?' in Hobbs, D. and May, T. (eds) *Interpreting the Field: Accounts of Ethnography*, Clarendon Press, Oxford.

Balbus, I. (1977) 'Commodity Form and Legal Form: An Essay on the 'Relative Autonomy' of the Law', *Law and Society*, 11, Winter, pp. 571-588.

Beirne, P. and Sharlet, R. (1982) 'Pashukanis and Socialist Legality', in Beirne, P. and Quinney, R. (eds) *Marxism and Law*, John Wiley and Sons, New York.

Belchem, J. (1996) *Popular Radicalism in Nineteenth-Century Britain*, Macmillan, London.

Benton, T. (1981) '"Objective" Interests and the Sociology of Power', *Sociology*, 15 (2), pp.161-184.

Bhaskar, R. (1978) *A Realist Theory of Science*, 2nd edition, Verso, London.

Cain, M. (1986) 'Realism, Feminism, Methodology and Law', *International Journal of the Sociology of Law*, 14, pp. 255-267.

Cain, M. (1990) 'Realist Philosophy and Standpoint Epistemologies or Feminist Criminology as a Successor Science', in Gelsthorpe, L. and Morris, A. (eds) *Feminist Perspectives in Criminology*, Open University Press, Milton Keynes.

Calhoun, G. (ed) (1992) *Habermas and the Public Sphere*, MIT Press, Cambridge, Massachusetts.

Chambliss, W. J. (1993) 'On Lawmaking' in Chambliss, W.J. and Zatz, M.S. (eds) *Making Law: The State, the Law and Structural Contradictions*, Indiana University Press, Indianapolis.

Clarke, S. (1988) *Keynesianism, Monetarism and the Crisis of the State*, Edward Elgar, Hants.

Clarke, S. (1991) 'The Value of Value: A Review of "Rereading Capital"' in Mohun, S. (ed) *Debates in Value Theory*, Macmillan, London.

Clarke, S. (1992) 'The Global Accumulation of Capital and the Periodisation of the Capitalist State Form', in Bonefeld, W., Gunn, R. and Psychopedis, K. (eds) *Open Marxism vol. 1: Dialectics and History*, Pluto Press, London.

Coleman, S. (1997) *Stilled Tongues: From Soapbox to Soundbite*, Porcupine Press, London.

Collier, A. (1994) *Critical Realism*, Verso, London.

Collins, H. (1982) *Marxism and Law*, Oxford University Press, Oxford.

Corrigan, P. and Sayer, D. (1981) 'How the Law Rules: Variations on Some Themes', in Marx, K. in Fryer, B., Hunt, A., McBarnet, D. and Moorhouse, B. (eds) *Law, State and Society*, Croom Helm, London.

Dwyer, K. (1982) *Moroccan Dialogues: Anthropology in Question*, J. Hopkins Press Ltd, London.

Fine, B. (1979) 'Law and Class', in Fine, B., Kinsey, R., Lea, J., Picciotto, S. and Young, J. (eds) *Capitalism and the Rule of Law: From Deviancy Theory to Marxism*, Hutchinson, London.

Finn, M. (1993) *After Chartism: Class and Nation in English Radical Politics, 1848-1874*, Cambridge University Press, Cambridge.

Freeman, A. D. (1982) 'Antidiscrimination Law: A Critical Review', in Kairys, D. (ed) *The Politics of Law: a Progressive Critique*, Pantheon Books, New York.

Fudge, J. and Glasbeek, H. (1992) 'The Politics of Rights: A Politics With Little Class', *Social and Legal Studies*, 1, pp. 45-70.

Gabel, P. and Feinman, J. (1982) 'Contract Law as Ideology', in Kairys, D. (ed) *The Politics of Law: a Progressive Critique*, Pantheon Books, New York.

Gatrell, V.A.C. (1994) *The Hanging Tree: Execution and the English People 1770 1868*, Oxford University Press, Oxford.

Geertz, C. (1993) *The Interpretation of Cultures*, Fontana Press, London.

Gramsci, A. (1986) *Selections from Prison Notebooks*, Lawrence and Wishart, London.

Gunn, R. (1989) 'Marxism and Philosophy: A Critique of Critical Realism', *Capital and Class*, no. 37, pp. 86-116.

Hay, D. (1975) 'Property, Authority and the Criminal Law' in Hay, D., Linebaugh, P., Rule, J., Thompson, E.P. and Winslow, C. *Albion's Fatal Tree: Crime and Society in Eighteenth-Century England*, Allen Lane, London.

Harrison, R. (1965) *Before the Socialists: Studies in Labour and Politics, 1861- 1881*, Routledge and Kegan Paul, London.

Herman, D. (1993) 'Beyond the Rights Debate', *Social and Legal Studies*, 2, pp.25-43.

Huggon, J. (ed) (1977) *Speakers' Corner: An Anthology*, Kropotkin's Lighthouse Publication, London.

Hunt, A. (1981) 'The Politics of Law and Justice', in Adlam, D. *et al.* (eds) *Politics and Power Four: Law, Politics and Justice*, Routledge and Kegan Paul, London.

Hunt, A. (1985) 'The Ideology of Law: Advances and Problems in Recent Applications of the Concept of Ideology to the Analysis of Law', *Law and Society Review*, 20, 1, pp.11-37.

Hunt, A. (1990) 'Rights and Social Movements: Counter-Hegemonic Strategies', *Journal of Law and Society*, 17(3) Autumn, pp. 309-328.

Jessop, B. (1990) *State Theory: Putting Capitalist States in their Place*, Polity Press, Cambridge.

Kairys, D. (1982) 'Freedom of Speech', in Kairys, D. (ed), *The Politics of Law: a Progressive Critique*, Pantheon Books, New York.

Kay, G. (1988) 'Right and Force: A Marxist Critique of Contract and the State', in Williams, M. (ed) *Value, Social Form and the State*, Macmillan, London.

Kay, G. and Mott, J. (1982) *Political Order and the Law of Labour*, Macmillan, Hampshire.

Kay, G. and Mott, J. (1984) 'Notes on the Law of Capital', *International Journal of the Sociology of Law* 12, pp. 261-270.

Kerruish, V. (1991) *Jurisprudence as Ideology*, Routledge, London.

Larrain, J. (1994) *Ideology and Cultural Identity: Modernity and the Third World Presence*, Polity Press, Cambridge.

Linebaugh, P. (1975) 'The Tyburn Riot Against the Surgeons', in Hay, D., Linebaugh, P., Rule, J., Thompson, E.P. and Winslow, C., *Albion's*

Fatal Tree: Crime and Society in Eighteenth-Century England, Allen Lane, London.

Linebaugh, P. (1991) *The London Hanged: Crime and Civil Society in the Eighteenth Century*, Penguin, London.

Lemaire, T. (1991) 'Anthropological Doubt', in Nencel, L. and Pels, P. (eds) *Constructing Knowledge: Authority and Critique in Social Science*, Sage, London.

Marx, K. (1966) *Capital,* vol. III, Progress Publishers, Moscow.

Marx, K. (1988) *Capital,* vol. I, Penguin, London.

Mattick, Jr., P. (1986) *Social Knowledge: An Essay on the Nature and Limits of Social Science*, Hutchinson, London.

Medvedev, P., Bakhtin, M. (1978) *The Formal Method in Literary Scholarship*, trans. by A. Wehrle, John Hopkins University Press, Baltimore.

Pashukanis, E. (1983) *Law and Marxism: A General Theory*, by Einhorn, B. (trans), Arthur, C. (ed), Pluto Press, London.

Pearson, G. (1993) 'Talking a Good Fight: Authenticity and Distance in the Ethnographer's Craft', in Hobbs, D. and May, T. (eds) *op cit.*, pp.vii-xx.

Picciotto, S. (1979) 'The Theory of the State, Class Struggle and the Rule of Law' in Fine, B. *et al.* (eds) *Capitalism and the Rule of Law: From Deviancy Theory to Marxism*, Hutchinson, London.

Postone, M. (1993) *Time, Labor and Social Domination*, Cambridge University Press, Cambridge.

Poulantzas, N. (1978) *State, Power, Socialism*, Verso, London.

Richardson, R. (1989) *Death, Dissection and the Destitute*, Pelican, London.

Santos, Boaventura De Sousa (1985) 'On Modes of Production of Law and Social Power', *International Journal of the Sociology of Law*, 13, pp. 299-336.

Sayer, A. (1992) *Method in Social Science: A Realist Approach* 2nd edition, Routledge, London.

Scholte, B. (1986) 'The Charmed Circle of Geertz's Hermeneutics: A neo-Marxist Critique', *Critique of Anthropology,* 6, 1, pp. 5-15.

Steiner, F. (1991) 'Introduction: Research as Self-Reflexivity, Self-Reflexivity as Social Process', in Steiner, F. (ed) *Research and Reflexivity*, Sage, London.

Sumner, C. (1979) *Reading Ideologies: An Investigation into the Marxist Theory of Ideology and Law*, Academic Press, London.

Thompson, E.P. (1980) *The Making of the English Working Class*, Penguin, London.

Urry, J. (1981) *The Anatomy of Capitalist Societies: The Economy, Civil Society and the State*, Macmillan, London.

Van Maanen, J. (1995) 'An End to Innocence: The Ethnography of Ethnography', in Van Maanen, J. (ed) *Representation in Ethnography*, Sage, London.

Warrington, R (1981) 'Pashukanis and the Commodity Form Theory', *International Journal of the Sociology of Law,* 9, pp. 1-22.

Weeks, J. (1981) *Capital and Exploitation*, Edward Arnold, London.

Weeks, J. (1997) 'The Law of Value and the Analysis of Underdevelopment', *Historical Materialism,* 1, Autumn, pp. 91-112.

Woodiwiss, A. (1985) 'A Theoretical Prologue to a Socialist Historiography of Labour Law: Law, Discourse and Transpositioning', *International Journal of the Sociology of Law,* 13, pp. 61-78.

Woodiwiss, A. (1990) *Social Theory After Postmodernism: Rethinking Production, Law and Class*, Pluto Press, London.

Woodiwiss, A. (1992) 'The Passing of Modernism and Labour Rights: Lessons from Japan and the United States', *Social and Legal Studies,* 1, pp. 477-491.

3 Accessing and analysing police murder files

Fiona Brookman

Introduction

This chapter addresses problems of access to, and qualitative analyses of police murder files. It is based on my PhD research into patterns and scenarios of masculine homicide and violence across England and Wales. Police murder files are a type of documentary source rarely used by researchers and, to the best of my knowledge, nothing has been published regarding the specific problems of using data contained in such files.

After setting out the reasons for using police murder file data in the research, I turn to the problems of accessing murder files. Whilst the issues discussed in the first half of the chapter are of particular importance when researching sensitive topics, such as homicide, they are still of relevance to other criminological research projects. Finally I move on to argue that researchers need to be aware that the data they analyse have undergone social construction and that this affects the manner in which one interprets and analyses the data.

Choosing data - why police murder files?

A range of data has been utilised in the research project. A large statistical data base, the 'Homicide Index' (1990-1994) was analysed to provide an initial insight into official patterns and volume of homicide across England and Wales. The vast majority of studies conducted into homicide use quantitative analyses in some form or another, particularly studies carried out in America, where it can sometimes seem as if quantitative forms of analysis are the only techniques or methods relied upon (Gibson, 1975; Silverman and Mukherjee, 1987; Strang, 1991; Wilbanks, 1995; Wolfgang, 1958). A good example of this can be found in the recently formed journal 'Homicide Studies' - an International and Interdisciplinary Journal. The four issues that comprised volume one of the journal in 1997 contained a total of nineteen articles, eleven of which relied exclusively on quantitative analyses to test hypotheses and assumptions about various forms of homicide. Only three articles relied exclusively on qualitative analyses of documentary material, such as police murder files and newspaper reports.

Clearly quantitative analyses are useful insofar as they provide valuable information regarding the patterns, trends and volume of homicide, notwithstanding problems of a 'dark figure' when relying upon statistical data (Coleman and Moynihan, 1996; Government Statisticians' Collective, 1979; Lewis, 1992; Maguire, 1997; White, 1995). In the case of homicide in England and Wales, the Home Office provide more information than would normally be made available in criminal offences, such as the circumstances or motive surrounding homicide, the relationship between victims and offenders and the method of killing. The drawback with such data become apparent when one wishes to gain rather more insight into this phenomenon. For example, the information available on the motives surrounding homicide are somewhat rudimentary, and are generally presented in the form of single word descriptions such as, rage, quarrel, jealousy or revenge. Such information, whilst useful as a starting point, raises many more questions than it is suited to answer. For example, what are the specific nature, or causes, of the quarrels that lead to homicide? Under what sorts of circumstances might people become jealous or harbor a grudge and ultimately kill? In order to answer such questions an alternative source of data, and an alternative form of analysis, preferably qualitative in nature, is required. Essentially then, quantitative analysis of the homicide index is not, on its own, sufficient to address theoretical questions about why certain people, under certain circumstances, become embroiled in lethal violence.

The search for more detailed information on homicide, led to the gathering and analysis of ninety five covering reports from police murder files. These reports were obtained from three different police force areas across England and Wales (the names and locations of these forces have been disguised for reasons of confidentiality), relating to the years 1994 and 1996. Covering reports form part of a much larger police murder file. Further details of the nature and content of police covering reports will be provided below, suffice it to say they comprise a condensed (though not un-detailed) version of the events surrounding the homicide and include details of offenders, victims, circumstances leading up to the homicide and previous histories of the victim and offender. The murder files are much more conducive to addressing in-depth questions about the circumstances of homicide, not least because it is a primary concern of police investigations to determine a motive for homicide and the surrounding circumstances in order to best determine what charge should be brought, if any, against a defendant (Daly and Wilson, 1988).

The important question that now arises, is to what extent is this alternative form of homicide data itself limited? This will be addressed later in the chapter, after considering some of the difficulties encountered in accessing the police files.

Access negotiations: entering the world of the murder squad

The ease, or difficulty, with which one is permitted access to sensitive data is dependent upon many factors, several of which appear to owe very little to the value of the research, and more to serendipity, determination and good negotiation skills. What follows is a brief account of my experiences of 'dealing with' police officers from three police forces across England and Wales.

Negotiating access to view police murder files proved to be a complex, dynamic and ongoing process, involving numerous forms of correspondence and contact, both formal and informal, with several different layers of hierarchy across each of the police force areas. Ultimately the negotiations that took place and the 'deals that were struck' between myself and officers at the respective forces were quite different, as was the manner in which the information was made available.

Negotiations began at Denton (a mixed force area comprising both urban and rural areas) where my supervisor initiated proceedings through a high ranking contact he had at the force. Informal discussion between the Detective Superintendent and my supervisor led to an agreement, in principle, that I would be permitted to view police murder files from the Denton Police Force Area. A formal letter of request was drawn up detailing the nature of the research and offering assurances of confidentiality. Approximately two weeks later I received a telephone call from a Detective Inspector who had been assigned the role of 'unearthing' (the significance of this term will be revealed in due course) the relevant murder files and co-ordinating my visits to the station to view the files. Some four weeks later, I viewed what was to be the first of many covering reports from police murder files.

At this early stage of the research I was under the impression that I had overcome a major hurdle, I was 'in', so to speak. However as the months passed it became evident that other obstacles would hinder the ease with which I would access the data. My preconceptions that police murder files would be neatly filed in some secured and centralised area for the respective forces could not have been further from the truth. The files were scattered across many different police stations, often buried beneath paperwork of the officer who last dealt with or was possibly still dealing with aspects of the case. Whilst I initially thought that this was a feature peculiar to the Denton Force I soon learnt that the situation was much the same in all three forces. Consequently I was put in a position of having to make frequent visits to the Denton force to view a few files then wait for extended periods of time until a few more had been located, whereupon I would return once more. Moreover I was put in the uncomfortable position of having to continually 'chase up' officers to retrieve additional files. Many of these officers were clearly very busy and would rather have not been elected as my aide. All in all it took a total of fourteen months to view all of the files at Denton and ultimately nine files were never viewed, primarily due to difficulties in locating the files.

Some different obstacles had to be overcome at Foxlee (also a mixed force area), the second force approached. Once again initial access was fairly straightforward. At my request the Chief Superintendent at Denton telephoned the Chief Superintendent at Foxlee on my behalf and put in a 'good word'. This was an important approach tactic since it allowed my role as a researcher to be communicated by one senior ranking officer to another and enhanced my credibility as a researcher. The manner in which the information was made available to me from the Foxlee force was quite different to Denton. The relevant information was extracted from the HOLMES database.

HOLMES (Home Office Large Major Enquiries System) is a computerised information storage and retrieval system which allows for all information emanating from any major enquiry to be stored, indexed, cross referenced and interrogated for investigative significance (Maguire and Norris, 1992, p.57). Many forces can recover information on all or most homicides using the HOLMES system, and this was the situation at Foxlee.[1]

For my purposes, HOLMES was used simply as a source of retrieving information in relation to known homicides committed in the Foxlee area during 1994 and 1996. An experienced officer trained in the use of this database would retrieve information in my presence and subsequently elaborate upon important issues where known. If the officer extracting the information was not familiar with a particular case, he (incidentally it was always a male officer and throughout the whole fieldwork period I never had any direct contact with a female officer) would contact an officer who had worked on the case, either in person or by telephone and I was then able to question the officer first hand about specific aspects of the case.

This method of collecting the data was considerably quicker than reading through covering reports and avoided the problems encountered at Denton of locating the covering reports. Only four visits to the Foxlee force were required to complete the collection of data. However the information obtained was not on a par with that from Denton, essentially because my access to covering reports was restricted. Whilst I managed to gather together most of the factual details required for each homicide, the cases reviewed from Foxlee were somewhat less comprehensive than from either Denton or Bridgewood, the largest force sampled, to which I now turn.

Bridgewood, a Metropolitan force, was not the first force of this kind to be approached. Having received the co-operation of two police forces I felt fairly confident in making an approach to a Metropolitan force 'alone' so to speak. A formal, written request was sent to the first Metropolitan force containing all the relevant details of the research and outlining successful access to both Foxlee and Denton and the Home Office data. I felt all these factors would enhance the likelihood of receiving a positive response. However, I quickly received a rejection letter essentially to the effect that the force was overloaded with requests for assistance with research. I was a little dismayed but not overly concerned as several alternative Metropolitan forces existed that could be contacted. My main concern however was that approaching any of these forces in the same way might also prove fruitless. An informal telephone conversation between a senior criminologist at Cardiff University and a friend of his, a Detective Chief Inspector at Bridgewood, ultimately resolved the issue. The D.C.I. was more than willing to co-operate and once again the 'ball was rolling'. After an exchange of letters and contracts, I was given access to police covering reports which, on this occasion, were photocopied and posted to my office at the university.

In summary, initial access to each of the forces which agreed to co-operate essentially succeeded as a result of requests by an established research acquaintance or a police officer, which would seem to suggest that 'who you know' is a crucial factor in opening up the gateway for research, particularly in such a sensitive area as homicide.

Many researchers have observed that access should not be thought of as an initial phase of entry to the research setting (Hammersley and Atkinson, 1995; Johnson, 1975). Rather it is best seen as involving an ongoing, if often implicit, process, in which the researcher's right to be present is continually renegotiated. In other words, access can be described, at the very least, as a two stage strategy[2] - 'getting in' and 'getting along' - the former referring to initial physical access, the latter to ongoing social access. The following section describes this latter phase.

In-house negotiations: reaffirming the research role

A number of different officers assisted me at each of the forces, particularly at the Foxlee force where each visit involved different officers accessing HOLMES on my behalf (and on one occasion, several different officers in one day). It was often the case that these officers were only provided with vague, rudimentary information regarding the purposes of the research and certainly none of them were provided with a copy of the formal letter of request sent to the force commander at the initial access stage. Consequently, I was sometimes met with a considerable degree of curiosity, scepticism and even distrust by some officers. I found myself having to answer a number of questions about my interest in homicide; why I had chosen to study this topic, what exactly I wanted the data for, what I intended to do with it and what I ultimately hoped to gain from 'all of this' (my research). Whilst my responses varied, depending upon the questions asked and my feeling for the degree of curiosity or distrust expressed by the individual officers, essentially I was careful to explain how and why my interest in the topic had developed, to reiterate that the data would be treated in strictest confidence and that I did not wish to be given any details that would specifically identify the individuals involved. I indicated that I was in no way concerned with the police investigation of homicide, rather in the circumstances surrounding and social dynamics of homicide. Finally, whilst keen to portray myself as a competent researcher. I simultaneously felt it was important to clearly acknowledge that they (the officers) were the experts on this matter from whom I hoped to learn something. This approach seemed to work in that any initial scepticism and distrust seemed to quickly abate and all of the officers emerged as accommodating and friendly. Clearly though this is a good example of the manner in which researchers have to renegotiate their right to be present in a particular research setting. So although my identity as a bona fide researcher had been accepted by the initial gatekeepers (high ranking police officers), it was often the case that I had to reaffirm my credibility and integrity to other officers throughout the process of data collection in order to harvest and maintain good relationships and also, to use Holdaway's phrase, 'to pierce their protective shields' (Holdaway, 1983, p.4).

51

The problems that previous researchers have encountered regarding suspicion and distrust among those they are studying were arguably more acute in the current research, despite the fact that I was not researching the police per se. The reasons for this would appear to revolve around the particular culture of the police force. Several researchers claim to have identified the existence of a 'cop' or 'canteen' culture which, amongst other features, incorporates characteristics such as suspiciousness, cynicism, internal solidarity and social isolation. (For comprehensive discussions see Holdaway, 1979; 1983; Reiner, 1992; Skolnick, 1966; Young, 1993). Whilst this is not the place to review in any detail the complexities of cop culture, it is clear that the aforementioned characteristics, in particular the insular nature of the police force, could play a role in increasing police officers distrust of the 'civilian researcher'.

Having outlined some of the difficulties encountered in securing the police file data, I now move on to consider a number of problems that emerged in 'making sense' of these data.

Police murder files as research data - fact or fiction!

As with any research method, documentary research raises a number of methodological problems.[3] Essentially, documents can be used in one of two ways; either as a resource *for* social research or as a topic *of* social research (Hakim, 1987; May, 1997). In other words, documents, such as police murder files or coroner's reports, can be used to learn about murder and death certification respectively (the relevant facts so to speak), or alternatively they can be used to learn something about the people who produce and maintain these records (Deutscher, 1973, p.10). In the latter instance it is not assumed that documents are neutral artefacts which independently report social reality (May, 1997, p.164). Rather, the researcher clearly acknowledges that documents are socially constructed and pays particular attention to issues such as who compiled the document and for what audience was it intended. As McDonnell (1986) notes, a fundamental feature of discourse (speech and writing) is that it is social, that is the words which are used and their meanings depend on where they were used, by whom and to whom.

The use of documents in the current research combined both approaches to analysis. Although initially police murder files were examined as a resource *for* the research (i.e. to gain an in-depth account of homicide across England and Wales), it quickly became apparent (not least due to the 'value laden' language used) that the files would have to be approached with caution and viewed in terms of the context in which they were written.

Hakim (1987, p.42) states that

Some understanding of the nature and original purpose of any set of records is important not only with reference to the quality, consistency and completeness of the data they provide, but also for the interpretations that can be placed on the results.

Similarly, Scott (1990, p.22) points out, the researcher must be aware of a document's credibility and conduct 'an appraisal of how distorted its contents are likely to be'. As already indicated, I was given access to Police Covering Reports (PCR's) as opposed to whole murder files. Police covering reports are an 'executive summary' of the circumstances surrounding a homicide. They are written by one or more of the senior officers who investigated the case and subsequently interviewed the suspect(s) and any witnesses. They range from anything between twenty to a hundred pages in length, depending essentially upon the size and complexity of the investigation and the number of witnesses questioned. Also some officers tend to go into considerably more depth than others when writing these reports. There are at least three significant aspects relating to the compilation of the P.C.R. that indicate its potentially biased nature.

In the first instance it is important to recognise that PCR's are written for a particular purpose and for a particular audience and as such can be viewed as attempts at persuasion. Covering reports must be supplied to the Crown Prosecution Service within ten weeks from the time that a suspect or suspects are charged with murder. Whilst these reports are not exclusively used in evidence (prosecution and defence barristers view complete murder files and form their own opinions of the case), for my purposes it was important to be aware of any possible biases within these reports.

Covering reports essentially represent a private communication between the police and 'their solicitors', the Crown Prosecution Service. They are not meant to be a communication for anyone else, and the defence are never given access to these documents. The evidence contained in the report is that which best supports the charge (of murder) and as such it presents the prosecution case in its strongest and most favourable light. Whilst the police cannot perversely ignore key evidence that does not support their case (for example a witness statement to the effect that the accused was at home with them at the time of the murder) they certainly are not required to present a complete or balanced representation of events. Specifically, the police do not have to present, in any detail, evidence from 'unused witnesses' that might in fact place the defendant in a favourable light. Ultimately, prosecuting lawyers receive subsequent reports that do point out in detail all the potential pitfalls of the prosecution case (in the form of unused materials and disclosure reports).

A second limitation with these reports relates to the particular authors of the reports. The P.C.R. is invariably the final phase in the process of the police murder investigation and its contents cannot be detached from the investigatory process that precedes it. Those same senior officers who attended the scene of the murder, talked to witnesses, friends and relatives of the deceased and of the suspect, and ultimately interviewed any suspects or witnesses, will have themselves written the murder report. Furthermore, those same officers will have been responsible for co-ordinating and directing the murder investigation. Consequently both emotional involvement in the murder investigation and responsibility for deciding what lines of enquiry to pursue will affect the manner in which the events are finally portrayed in police murder files. Similarly, the officers' previous experience of suspects, witnesses and 'criminals' generally will colour their judgement in a number of subtle and complex ways. Clearly, it is not unreasonable to assume that the evidence portrayed in such files will be somewhat biased or slanted towards the officers' views of events as formulated throughout the investigative process itself. Discussions with individual officers throughout the collection of the files confirmed this. The following comments taken from police covering reports illustrate some of the biases I have been discussing.[4]

> Joanne Smith is a juvenile without previous. She is not a junkie and in my opinion is the only one of the occupants of 44 High Street that has a grasp of time and full reality.

Clearly the officer's view of 'junkies' and persons with previous convictions would have led him to have placed more reliance upon Joanne's statement (a key witness in this case) as compared to the rest of the household, all of whom were potentially equally valid witnesses to the crime. This in turn may have affected the manner in which the investigation proceeded.

In another case the police officer writing the report has clearly formed the opinion that the victim provoked his own demise, based upon his behaviour and actions both at the time of the murder and on previous occasions. The officer makes reference to a catalogue of events which

54

show the victim to be little short of a drunken, crazed animal and which support the suggestion that 'the accused in this case was in fact petrified of the victim'.

In a further case a police officer ends the report

This was a cold-blooded, pre-meditated execution, planned and prepared. The defendant could easily have physically assaulted the victim bearing in mind his larger stature.

These cases illustrate, in different ways, the manner in which the police try to portray a particular message to the reader. In the second of the above three cases, the officer is obviously of the opinion that the least severe penalty possible would be appropriate. In the latter case, the use of words such as planned and pre-meditated, coupled with the emotive term 'execution', mirror those fitting of a conviction for murder.

Whether or not one agrees with the opinions documented by the officers is of course inconsequential. The important point is that police covering reports are not neutral documents and the researcher must be acutely aware of this. In sum, as Scott (1990) suggests, documents cannot be usefully employed in social research if they are thought of as wholly disconnected from the authors intentions.

Aside from these obvious problems of subjectivity and bias, in what is a document essentially designed to convince the C.P.S. to prosecute a case (as described to me by several police officers), there is also a question of the validity of the data in terms of factual detail. Even if one were to assume that the police reported the case neutrally, they are in a position of having to rely (in some cases exclusively) upon information supplied to them by witnesses and suspects (in some rare cases the victim may survive for long enough to provide a statement) in order to try and reconstruct the events that led up to the homicide (physical/forensic evidence is also very important in building a case). The problem of course is that they are often dealing with individuals who are not in a position to accurately report events, as a result of being intoxicated at the time or under the influence of drugs. Also some witnesses have reason to distort the facts (they may be friends of family members of a suspect or of the victim). Alternatively, witnesses may wish to distance themselves from what has gone on and minimise their role in the events (for example, where they have handed an offender a weapon or 'egged' on a fight). Even where witnesses have no reason to deliberately distort the facts, there are numerous problems with eye-witness testimony (Wells and Loftus, 1984; Ross et al., 1994). Events can be so emotionally charged that accurate recall and reporting is

55

problematic. Few of the reports I analysed were free from contradiction. Vital ' witnesses often presented very different accounts of what had occurred leaving it up to the police to decide whose version was most accurate.

As my analysis of the covering reports progressed I found myself developing a somewhat cynical approach to the contents. I continually questioned assumptions made by the officers who had written the reports (not unlike the cynical and sceptical views of the officers in respect of certain witnesses and suspects they questioned). In short, the frequently biased nature of the police covering reports presented me with certain dilemmas. How far should these documents be relied upon as meaningful representations of the homicides to which they refer? How might the evidence contained within the police documents be balanced with additional information?

A number of possible alternatives were considered, such as viewing the police prosecution brief in full (complete murder files), conducting interviews with witnesses from the cases myself, or viewing solicitors' files or court transcripts. Each of these alternatives posed certain problems however. For example, interviewing witnesses was not a feasible option for two reasons. Firstly, *sub judice* rules prohibit witnesses from discussing any aspects of the case until trial completion. Certainly many of the cases I analysed had not been resolved at court. Even in those cases that were complete, the mechanisms necessary to identify witnesses and receive their permission to be interviewed would have been extremely complicated and cumbersome and simply not feasible within the time scale to which I was obliged to work. Viewing the police prosecution brief in full was another option considered. This would permit closer analysis of 'raw' information, and would avoid the problems of it having been filtered by the police interpretation. Of course, whether or not I would be able to produce a less biased or more balanced picture of events myself, is questionable. These files are vastly larger than the PCR's that I viewed; they average four inches in thickness and are a very cumbersome document. As well as the covering report they contain charge/summons sheets, full criminal histories (where appropriate) of the victim and suspects, transcripts of witness and suspect statements in full, expert witness statements (such as forensic scientists, fingerprint and D.N.A. experts) and all the relevant exhibits (scenes of crime photographs and photographs of injuries to the deceased and so forth). Discussions with several officers regarding the possiblity of my viewing these files confirmed my suspicions, it would be very difficult if not impossible to achieve, not least because the problems encountered in locating the covering reports would become even more significant in the case of complete files.

The final decision taken was to conduct in-depth, qualitative interviews with men convicted of murder, manslaughter and serious but non-lethal violence (such as grievous bodily harm, wounding with intent and attempted homicide) towards other men. The rationale for this decision was based upon the work of Athens (1980) who argues that the viewpoint of the person whose actions are under study always be explicitly taken into account in explaining their conduct (Athens, 1980, p.14). In other words, it is essential that one considers, at least in part, the act of homicide from the point of view of the perpetrator. The decision to include violent men, as opposed to just men who had committed murder or manslaughter, was based on a number of factors, not least the fact that homicide and non-lethal violence share many similarities and it is often more the result of chance and situational circumstances as to whether a violent assault becomes lethal (Pokorny, 1990). Having now completed this final phase of data collection it has become apparent that a number of other methodological issues will need to be addressed. In much the same way as the researcher has to make some value judgement about the credibility of a document, so too

> [A]n interviewer has to form a judgement about how knowledgeable or truthful their informants are
> (O'Connell Davidson and Layder, 1994, p.188)

In other words, interview data are themselves subject to all forms of bias and distortion, albeit rather distinct from the kinds of biases contained in the police files, and raise numerous problems of interpretation (Bogdan and Taylor, 1975; Chirban, 1996; Dean and Foote Whyte, 1988; Jupp, 1989; Kvale, 1996; O'Connell Davidson and Layder, 1994).

In conclusion, police covering reports are biased to an unknown degree and furthermore contain no account of the events from the point of view of the victim - one of the central 'actors' in the homicide. Unfortunately, this is the case with all data on this particular phenomenon, which is one of the reasons why the homicide researcher must be acutely aware of the credibility of the accounts they chose to rely upon in gaining insight into this particular form of violence. Essentially whatever one ultimately analyses is a socially constructed narrative which may or may not be an accurate reflection of events.

Concluding comments

Some of the difficulties that arise in using documentary material to research homicide in England and Wales have been considered in this chapter. Police murder files are one source of information about homicide. Like any data, they have their limitations. As my experiences demonstrate, I was forced to consider carefully the boundaries of these data and supplement them with in-depth, qualitative interviews with violent men in order to explore violence from a very different perspective; that of the perpetrators as opposed to the police.

On a more general level, this chapter has illustrated that researchers need to be constantly aware of the boundaries of the data that they are working with and the techniques of analyses they use. Sometimes it is tempting not to ask the right questions because the data, or analyses, will not permit it. Instead, as researchers, we must be prepared to search for the kinds of data and adopt the particular forms of analyses that permit us to address the most useful range of research questions. This, after all, is part and parcel of what it means to conduct interesting, challenging and useful criminological research.

I would like to express my thanks to several police officers (they know who they are) who provided me with frank and informed information regarding the nature, content and purpose of Police Covering Reports.

Notes

1. HOLMES was initially used in only the most complex and challenging serious crimes (such as murder, rape, armed robberies and assaults), particularly those for which there was no obvious suspect, little evidence on which to base an enquiry and for those cases in which possible links could be made with other similar or different crimes. However, many forces now routinely adopt HOLMES for all or most murder enquiries regardless of the complexity of the case. In these cases HOLMES is not used to its full capacity, rather a shortened version of HOLMES is utilised.

2. Additionally, in ethnographic research, there often exists a third stage that has been termed 'getting out', which refers to some of the issues that confront a researcher when leaving a research site after extended periods of stay. This particular aspect was not relevant to the current research.

3.	There exists a substantial literature on theoretical approaches to documentary analysis. For example; Cicourel, 1976; Forster, 1994; Jupp and Norris, 1994; Platt, 1981; Plummer, 1990.

4.	Names, addresses and so forth have been altered within these quotes to protect the identity of individuals involved.

References

Athens, L. (1980) *Violent Criminal Acts and Actors: A Symbolic Interactionist Study,* Routledge and Kegan Paul, London.

Bogdan, R. and Taylor, S.J. (1975) *Introduction to Qualitative Research Methods: A Phenomenological Approach to the Social Sciences,* John Wiley & Sons, London.

Chirban, J.T. (1996) *Interviewing in Depth: The Interactive-Relational Approach,* Sage, London.

Cicourel, A. (1976) *The Social Organisation of Juvenile Justice,* Heinemann, London.

Coleman, C. and Moynihan, J. (1996) *Understanding Crime Data: Haunted by the Dark Figure,* Open University Press, Philadelphia.

Daly. M. and Wilson, M. (1988) *Homicide,* Aldine De Gruyter, New York.

Dean, J.P. and Foote Whyte. W. (1988) 'How do you know if the informant is telling the truth?', in Bynner, J. and Stribley, K.M. (eds), *Social Research: Principles and Procedures,* Longman, Essex.

Deutscher, I. (1973) *What We Say/What We Do,* Scott, Foresman, Glenview, Ill.

Forster, N. (1994) The Analysis of Company Documents, in Cassell, C. and Symon, G. (eds), *Qualitative Methods in Organizational Research: A Practical Guide,* Sage, London.

Gibson, E. (1975) *Homicide in England and Wales 1967-1971,* Home Office Research Study, No 31, HMSO, London.

Government Statisticians' Collective (1979) 'How Official Statistics are Produced: Views from the Inside', in Irvine, J., Miles, I., and Evans, J. (eds), *Demystifying Social Statistics,* Pluto Press, London.

Hakim, C. (1987) *Research Design: Strategies and Choices in the Design of Social Research,* Allen & Unwin Ltd., London.

Hammersley, M., and Atkinson, P. (1995) *Ethnography: Principles in Practice,* Routledge, London.

Holdaway, S. (1979) *The British Police,* Edward Arnold, London.

Holdaway, S. (1983) *Inside the British Police,* Blackwell, Oxford.

Johnson, J.M. (1975) *Doing Field Research,* Free Press, New York.

Jupp, V. (1989) *Methods of Criminological Research,* Unwin Hyman, London.

Jupp, V. and Norris, C. (1994) 'Traditions in Documentary Analysis', in Hammersley, M. (ed), *Social Research: Philosophy, Politics and Practice,* Sage, London.

Kvale, S. (1996) *Interviewing: An Introduction to Qualitative Research Interviewing,* Sage, California.

Lewis, C. (1992) 'Crime Statistics: Their Use and Misuse', *Social Trends,* 22, pp. 13-23, Central Statistical Office, Home Office, London.

Maguire, M. (1997) 'Crime Statistics, Patterns, and Trends: Changing Perceptions and their Implications', in Maguire, M., Morgan. R. and Reiner. R. (eds), *The Oxford Handbook of Criminology,* 2nd Edition, Clarendon Press, Oxford.

Maguire, M., and Norris, C. (1992) *The Conduct and Supervision of Criminal Investigations*, The Royal Commission on Criminal Justice, Research Study No 5., HMSO, London.

May, T. (1997) *Social Research: Issues, Methods and Process,* Open University Press, Philadelphia.

McDonnell, D. (1986) *Theories of Discourse: An Introduction,* Blackwell, Oxford.

O'Connell Davidson, J. and Layder, D. (1994) *Methods, Sex and Madness,* Routledge, London.

Platt, J. (1981) *'Evidence and Proof in Documentary Research: 1. Some Specific Problems of Documentary Research',* Sociological Review, 29 (1), pp. 31-52.

Plummer, K. (1990) *Documents of Life: An Introduction to the Problems and Literature of a Humanistic Method,* George Allen and Unwin, London.

Pokorny, A.D. (1990) 'A Comparison of Homicide, Aggravated Assault, Suicide, and Attempted Suicide', in Weiner, N., Zahn, A. and Sagi, R. (eds), *Violence: Patterns, Causes, Public Policy,* Harcourt Brace College Publishers, London.

Reiner, R. (1992) *The Politics of the Police,* Wheatsheaf, Hemel Hempstead.

Ross, D.F., Read, J.D. and Toglia, M.P. (eds), (1994) *Adult Eyewitness Testimony: Current Trends and Developments,* Press Syndicate of the University of Cambridge, New York.

Sapsford, R. and Jupp, V. (1996) *Data Collection and Analysis,* Sage, London.

Scott, J. (1990) *A Matter of Record*, Polity Press, Cambridge.

Silverman, R.A. and Mukherjee, S.K. (1987) 'Intimate Homicide: An Analysis of Violent Social Relationships' *Behavioural Sciences and the Law*, 5 (1), pp. 37-47.

Skolnick, J. (1966) *Justice Without Trial*, Wiley, New York.

Strang, H. (1991) *Homicides in Australia 1989-199,* Australian Institute of Criminology, Canberra.

Wells, G.L. and Loftus, E.F. (eds), (1984) *Eyewitness Testimony: Psychological Perspectives,* Cambridge University Press, London.

White, P. (1995) 'Homicide', in Walker, M. (ed), *Interpreting Crime Statistics,* Clarendon Press, Oxford.

Wilbanks, W. (1995) 'Homicide in Singapore', *International Journal of Comparative and Applied Criminal Justice.* Spring 1995, 19 (1).

Wolfgang, M.E. (1958) *Patterns in Criminal Homicide,* Patterson Smith, Montclair, New Jersey.

Wolfgang, M.E. (1981) 'Confidentiality in Criminological Research and Other Ethical Issues', *Criminology,* 72 (1), pp. 345-361.

Young, M. (1993) *In the Sticks: Cultural Identity in a Rural Police Force,* Clarendon Press, Oxford.

4 Social constructions of violence against the police

Mike Levi and Lesley Noaks

Introduction

I feel no shame about hitting coppers

(Paul aged 19)

My friends loved it, none of us like the police, we all feel coppers should be followed home and put down

(David aged 24)

This chapter will examine the social construction of one part of 'the crime problem' - assaults against the police. Following the legal terminology, reference will be made to the offence as 'assault police'. It draws upon qualitative research conducted in a single police force area, supplemented by observations in other areas. The research was conducted in the late 1980s as a direct response to an increasing focus on the issue of violence directed toward police officers. Increased attention to the issue was reflected in the publication of a force league table by Police Review - a national police journal published weekly - of the relative risk of officers being assaulted (Police Review, 1987). This represented the first attempt at collating national statistics on assaults against the police. A number of police forces did not participate in the survey of assault rates, primarily because no force statistics were routinely gathered and available for analysis. Following publication of the survey results, the police force identified as having one of the highest levels of risk to officers elected to undertake a research project to explore in greater depth the nature of the problem in their area. Against that background this chapter will discuss the organisational influences which can impact on research methodologies, interpretation of findings and responses to outcomes. As Hughes (1996 p.61) suggests, research 'does not take place in a political and moral vacuum'. With this in mind we discuss the ways in which such contexts can undermine and put in jeopardy the efforts of the researcher to produce 'objective' accounts. Conducting research within organisations can produce findings which lack fit with the institutional agenda. While in this case, this was a problem in respect of a policing organisation, it can equally arise in other settings such as prisons, schools and health departments. The chapter will also address how the issue of police directed violence was constructed nationally, including the influence of the media on both local and national constructions.

Background to the research

Having been publicly identified as a high risk area for police officers, the major strategic response by senior police managers in 'Aggro force' was the commissioning of an independent research project. Following their placement at the top of the league table for police assaults, such violence was depicted as a new and emerging problem, requiring innovative strategies to combat it. Research funding was secured from the Home Office Police Requirements Support Unit and an independent researcher was appointed to facilitate gaining both the victim and assailant's perspective. The case was made by those commissioning the research that internal studies of the problem would be one-sided and partial in their focus. The broad aim of the project was to construct profiles of the offenders and police officers involved in assaults and to review the dynamics which led up to the point of aggression. In adopting this approach it was recognised that violence is an interpersonal phenomenon which is over-simplified by making a sharp distinction between the roles of perpetrator and victim. As Toch (1969) argued, violence is at at least a two man game and the interaction between the two parties will often be intricate and complex.

The research team consisted of two university based researchers and a police officer seconded to the project. A decision was made to locate the project on the university site to confirm the independent status of the project with both police officer victims and alleged assailants. Involving a police officer in the project did however provide the researchers with a significant gatekeeper into the typically closed culture of policing (Reiner, 1992).

A range of research strategies were adopted to diversify the channels by which data was gathered. Drawing on multiple data sources was felt to be particularly pertinent to the project in view of the brief that the research should extend beyond official accounts of the problem and uniquely combine victim and perpetrator perspectives. Research strategies included a proforma completed by individual police officers as soon as possible after the assault against them, which provided basic information on features of the event and their perspective on the incident. Face to face interviews were undertaken with a sample of alleged assailants to capture their view of the incident. In these interviews a semi-structured approach was adopted using open-ended questions to avoid an overly restricted stance. Respondents were talked through the incidents and actively encouraged to provide their personal viewpoint on the alleged violence that had occurred. Offenders were contacted by letter and asked to take part in the study and from the outset the tone of the letter sought to emphasise the independent status of the research and the importance of the respondent's personal perspective.

> I am a researcher from Cardiff University studying incidents which have resulted in a police officer being injured, however trivially, and irrespective of whether or not the injury was justified. What tends to get reported in the papers and television is the official police view, which obviously mainly reflects *their* ideas about what happened. But the aim of *my* study is to look at these incidents from the viewpoint of those who are alleged to have been responsible for the injury, and I would be very grateful to have the opportunity of listening to *your* version of what happened in your case.

The research also included shadowing of police officers by the independent researcher, particularly on evening and night shifts, providing the opportunity to observe the dynamics of public order incidents which typically preceded assaults. Finally the research included an analysis of print media coverage of offences of assault against police officers to ascertain how such outlets depicted the offence. In the case of the media we were particularly interested in whether there was any suggestion of police victims contributing to their own victimisation, a stance which has been adopted in respect of other categories of victim of violent crime (Levi, 1997). In summary, while the research strategy included some quantitative elements (such as violence rates in different parts of the force, to be correlated with demographic variables), the focus of the project was primarily qualitative research with the overarching aim of gaining authentic accounts of the problem of assault police, drawing on the experiences of both police officers and their assailants.

The emergence of assaults against the police as a social problem

Before moving on to discuss the constraints experienced in conducting research in organisational settings and our findings, we will review the factors which underpinned the recognition of assault police as a social problem at this point in time. In focusing on this issue we seek to highlight the frequently inescapable relationship between research and policy. A number of pertinent questions came to mind which provided an important backdrop to the design of the project and its methodology. Were we being asked to carry out this study because police targeted violence was an increasing problem? Were front line police officers less willing to tolerate victimisation and demanding greater support from managers? Were senior police managers seeking to highlight victimisation of police officers as a means of bolstering public support? These and other related questions helped to define the parameters of the research and directly influenced the methodologies that were adopted. As independent researchers invited into an organisation to investigate a specific issue it was important that we remained alert to the broad policy context that provided a backdrop to our investigations.

The mythology of recency: the golden age of police-public harmony

Recent attention to the issue of violence directed towards the police tended to infer that this is a new and emerging social problem - a particular product of recent violent times. A 'golden-ageist' view is regularly adopted with past police-public relations depicted as overwhelmingly trouble-free and amicable with aggressive, forceful policing only needing to rear its ugly head on rare occasions. In reality, however, the patchiness of historical records on rates of assault against police officers makes it impossible to state with any certainty that the trend is an increasing one. While media attention may confirm the impression that there is a growing problem, it remains debatable whether the police face any more violence in carrying out their duties than they have done in the past. The work of sceptical historians and sociologists (Gatrell, 1980, 1990; Pearson, 1983) provides ample evidence that attacks against the police and violent encounters between the police and the general public are not confined to the modern era. In common with many other forms of criminal victimisation, measuring trends in the incidence of offences of assault police is severely hampered by the unknown elements related to the size of the 'dark figure' of unrecorded crimes. Apparent increases in the levels of reported assault by police officers may be as related to changes in reporting behaviour as much as real changes in the levels of crime and risk. Research evidence gleaned from our shadowing of personnel suggested that new, young recruits, often with a good standard of education on entry to the force, were less prepared to tolerate aggressive reponses on the part of the public as part of the job. Whereas being able to handle oneself on the street and related minimisation of danger have traditionally been core elements in the macho subculture of policing, our research suggested that changes in the profile of police personnel, including but certainly not exclusively the recruitment of more women, had impacted on the attitude to assault police.

While it would not be defensible from our evidence to weight the relative importance of the factors discussed, it can be argued that a combination of these elements contributed to the concentrated spate of force investigations of the vulnerability of officers to physical attack and a consequent promotion of violence against the police as a social problem. Increased attention to the issue represents a definite shift of position by senior staff. Immediately prior to the research exercise undertaken by Police Review, force recording procedures were inadequate to the point that many forces were unable to provide data on the number of officers experiencing an attack, reflecting, we would suggest, the minimal significance with which the issue was viewed. Since that time, with the backing of the Home Office, forces have devoted resources to monitoring the extent of the issue and in some cases undertaken studies of the problems faced in their force, attempting to identify causes, trends and patterns of attack. The regularity with which, over the last decade, police forces have prioritised the issue of assaults on their officers is indicative that there has been a universal movement toward acknowledging the issue as a core problem for the police and its depiction as a related problem for the rest of society. Violence towards the police is increasingly portrayed as a modern phenomenon caused by the recent general decline in standards of everyday life. The stance of the police force in which the research was undertaken is reflected in their introduction to 'The Survey of Assaults on Police Officers in 1986' where it was stated that 'willingness to assault police officers when performing their duty is further evidence of a decline in social and legal norms and a total lack of respect of the law'. Public statements by politicians have echoed police concern and fuelled the moral panic that police-targeted violence is a growing problem symptomatic of an increasingly lawless and oppositional society.

One might suggest that it is easy to see the organisational morale value of senior officers expressing concern about assaults against police officers, who are almost always below the rank of inspector. Such concern acts as a solidarity-affirming factor which symbolises the harmony of interests within the police against the common enemy, i.e. the *non* law-abiding public and 'vested interest' groups. It might be expected that the lower ranks would interpret this as altruistic senior management concern about their being assaulted. There is no direct benefit to their superiors whose performance indicators do not include lowering such assaults in the way that they include improving clear-up rates for (recorded) crime. However, given that it is so functional for senior police to express concern about assaults on their junior officers, it seems appropriate to pose the standard question for all functionalist accounts and ask why media campaigns and such allied matters as the collation of nation-wide statistics on assaults did not begin in earnest prior to 1987? Are there any reasons why complaints about assaults became more functional in the late 1980s, or is the 'control wave' simply an historical accident? We had in mind the analysis of Hall et al. (1978) of the reasons for media and police focus on 'mugging', which suggested that the interests of (a) the police in constructing a black picture of the moral identity of Afro-Caribbeans, to justify their intended 'Operation Swamp' arrest strategy, and (b) the media, whose pre-existing stereotypes of black youth combined with routine dependence for their stories on friendly relationships with the police, together led to a moral panic about 'black mugging'. Access to police officers, at all levels of the hierarchy, facilitated our exploration of police constructions of assault police. Media perspectives were explored through interviews with local journalists and content analysis of national and local print media accounts of violent incidents involving police officers as both victims and perpetrators. The timescale for the content analysis was January to December 1989, the period for which we collected force data on assaults. In this way, we could test what the journalists told us about their coverage.

Mobilising the media

Relationships between police and media representatives always carry a potential for tension. Disregarding any pro-'law and order' ideological biases on the part of media proprietors, there is no conflict if the media are content to reproduce the standard diet of organisation-promoting (and, sometimes, personal career-serving) public relations stories fed by individual police and police press officers. (For general literature on crime news see Ditton and Duffy, 1983; Ericson et al., 1989; Reiner, 1997b). The conflict arises when feature or news stories are written (or researched) that contain any serious criticisms.[1] Discussions with journalists and television producers make it clear that national and local news media are principally interested in stories that portray the police in a sympathetic way as *victims*

67

rather than as *examples* of the 'yobbo tendency'. This is supported by the sorts of stories that appear both in the local and national press (whose identities we have also anonymised for data protection reasons and to preserve the anonymity of our force sample).

Our analysis of local press coverage of violence involving the police shows that it is generally supportive of their role in doing order-maintaining 'dirty work' on behalf of 'society as a whole'. Violence against the police is portrayed as an outcome of 'bad attitudes' by assailants against neutral agents of society who are 'just doing their job', rather than of an interaction process in which the attribution of blame is in any way problematic. In terms of balance, during 1989, the Wessex Express carried 27 stories about assaults *against* the police, compared with 9 stories alleging assaults *by* the police. In terms of allegations of police-press conspiracy or deliberate pro-police bias by the media, not too much should be made of this imbalance: these stories almost invariably reflect court cases, high-profile incidents of disorder, or annual reports of Chief Constables or of local justices' Licensing Committees, where issues such as the relationship between licenses to sell alcohol and violent crime can crop up. Reporting of the kind favoured by local and national crime reporters in turn reflects the way cases are presented in court and the hierarchy of credibility there which traditionally favours police evidence against that from the 'rough' working class (who are the normal physical opponents of the police). Since far more cases of assault *against* than assault *by* the police are brought to court, it is hardly surprising that the media reporting follows that distribution.

Perhaps more interesting - though no more surprising - is the fact that the style of coverage is far more negative about assaults *against* the police than about those *by* the police. Emotive adjectives and verbs are absent from the headlines on the latter, but are common in the former, e.g. 'Police battered in Christmas assaults' (29/12/89); '"Terror attack" four jailed' (14/10/89); 'Police swamped by tide of night attacks' (8/8/89); 'CS gas used against affray police' (12/6/89); and 'Night-time hell for the front-line boys in blue' (*Southern Post* 9/4/89).

A fairly typical example of the 'police as victim' focus of a local feature headline is Mental scars of the beaten-up bobbies (*Wessex Express*, 22/1/89).

On assaults *by* the police, the press seem careful not to be seen as anti-police, using words like 'allege' and 'claim' more often, and balancing the report more soberly. A good example was the headline 'Police assault claims increase' (*Wessex Express*, 13/12/89). This was based on the Annual Report of the Constabulary, and noted that 'more complaints about alleged assault on the public have been notched up by the Aggro Police

Force this year than last, but the overall number of complaints have dropped.' ('Other complaints' - where the reduction occurred - relate to more minor incivilities, but this is not specified in the article.) The assaults issue is more than just an expedient basis for a claim for greater resources. It has also the combined symbolic and instrumental function of asserting crime victims demands for general and special deterrence and/or for just deserts. Furthermore, this category of crime victims - the police - is making the special claim on our sympathies that - albeit that they are paid extra precisely because of the fact that they face the risk of violence - they are being hurt in the course of a job whose purpose is to protect 'society as a whole'. Our analysis of media depictions of the issue of assault police suggests that they have readily responded to police campaigns to promote and prioritise the issue as evidence of general social decay and that their style of reporting is generally supportive of presenting the police in a positive light, as the injured party. This supportive attitude is reinforced by the dependence of local news media on police sources for cheap and easy news material and access to authoritative 'primary definers' (Hall et al., 1978; Schlesinger and Tumber, 1994).

Problematising police targeted violence

Going beyond the influence of the media, our analysis of the issue of assault police and its increasing promotion as a social problem suggests that a range of factors combined at this point in time contributing to the upsurge in official concern regarding police directed violence. Once the issue of police targeted violence had begun to appear on media and public agendas, as well as addressing it as an internal issue, senior police managers saw fit to take every opportunity to focus attention on the increased risks faced by officers in their day-to-day work. Annual reports of police forces and other public statements make regular reference to the unacceptable level of violence encountered by officers as they go about their duties. If such public statements by managers regarding the risks and threats faced by their officers were intended to play a significant solidifying function at an organisational level, what was the climate of feeling which required the public representation of the police as a force under siege?

Our perspective is that it is no coincidence that such public relations exercises coincide with an era of declining public confidence in the police (Elliott and Dowds, 1989). By the late 1980s the police were facing increasing criticism of their tactics and methods, not unrelated to the emerging miscarriages of justice and the disbandment of the West Midlands Serious Crime Squad (Reiner, 1992). Both national and local crime surveys began to demonstrate an increased tendency for the public to be critical of the police, citing, amongst other factors, an inadequate response to crime. It is interesting to note that declining public support was particularly acute amongst groups which had traditionally been the mainstay of police support. The crisis of confidence and 'police bashing' began to emerge in Middle England and was no longer solely the prerogative of the disaffected and those characterised as the loony left. In the light of such trends, the police organisationally have an investment in representing themselves as the vulnerable 'thin blue line' defending law and order and holding the dangerous classes at bay. Furthermore the image of an over-stretched police force struggling to keep an upper hand is a powerful lever to reinforce claims on scarce government resources, particularly financial support. In these ways, the situation faced by police forces, vis-à-vis assaults against officers, can be used as an important part of a counter-defensive strategy and a means of promoting the good work done by police officers against the odds. The potential audiences for such messages are many and varied but by our analysis would include the Home Office, local police authorities, the general public and rank and file police officers. The pragmatic message for the researcher is that those sponsoring projects within their organisation will often not have a neutral view of the messages emanating from the research process. In particular, where outcomes are seen to reflect negatively on the organisation, sponsors may seek to block dissemination of research findings. Even once access has been gained to institutions or organisations, researchers need to be alert to the sponsors agenda and their particular investment in subsequent findings. We shall now provide a summary of our research findings and describe the response of some senior officers to the project recommendations.

Official/unofficial accounts and contested meanings

Our research findings identified that, in common with most other forms of offending, especially violent offending (Levi, 1997), the typical assailant was young and male. He was likely to have a previous criminal record, although not necessarily for a violent offence. He associated with people who had been involved in similar confrontations with the police and who were therefore likely to support his actions. There was a strong possibility that he would be unemployed, with an unemployment rate of 60 per cent among the offenders. Those in employment tended to hold low status jobs. For all offenders it is not difficult to envisage a shared value system characterised by lack of purpose, absence of long term goals and a general feeling that society has little to offer.

Turning to the police officers involved, the group most vulnerable to assault were uniformed constables. Amount of experience did not prove to be a significant factor in reducing the probability of an assault and the largest percentage of officers was drawn from those with between five and ten years service. This fact disproved a long held in-house myth that young, inexperienced officers were particularly at risk and that actions against them served to inflate assault rates. Female officers were found to be as much at risk as their male colleagues and were assaulted in direct proportion to their numbers in the force. Detective duties proved to be comparatively less hazardous, reflecting limited involvement of CID officers in confrontational public order work.

The majority of assaults occurred, or were at least initiated, in a public place, such as on the street or in licensed premises. The use of alcohol was a pervasive feature of incidents, reinforcing the popularly accepted link between alcohol and aggressive, violent behaviour (HMSO, 1989). However our findings on the drink patterns of offenders suggested that to go out drinking and consume a significant amount of alcohol was a normative leisure activity and means of having a good time. Even those who do assault the police after drinking, often drink heavily without assaulting the police. Consequently, the view that drinking *causes* assaults is too crude, even though alcohol may serve as a catalyst. In terms of the dynamics of the incident, confrontation between the police and their assaulters regularly led on from 'trouble' or 'bother' with other individuals. A common scenario was for the arrival of the police to result in redirection of anger and aggression towards them.

As required by our research brief, our analysis of the dynamics of violent incidents, with both victims and perpetrators, produced accounts which went beyond official versions of the problem of assault police. Prior to this piece of work, not only had limited research been undertaken in this area, but that work which had been done took account solely of the authorised line provided by 'primary definers' and depicted the police unambiguously as victims. This construction of assaults was expedient for the police, at an organisational level, in seeking to portray itself as devoid of any active contribution to the violent event and on the receiving end of unwarranted abuse. Such constructions, which typically depicted police officers as playing a passive or neutral role, were put in jeopardy by the research findings emerging from this project. In particular such accounts were challenged by our finding that the attitude and approach adopted by police officers frequently did contribute to how events were played out and

71

whether violence occurred. In the same way that victim precipitation has been a contentious issue in other areas of victimisation, such as rape (Amir, 1971), critical questions arose as to what extent assaulted police officers contributed to the violent outcome. While a minority of assaulted officers experienced 'out of the blue' attacks with no prior interaction with their assailants, in a majority of cases the assaults were embedded in an ongoing contact. Some assailants' accounts described how in interactions with the police, overly assertive and aggressive attitudes on the part of officers had led to an escalation of tension and contributed to the violent outcome. Some officers also experienced multiple 'victimisations' in the research period, with a maximum of five assaults against a single officer in the twelve month period under study. Such findings contributed to the researchers' conclusions that an understanding of the problem of assault police needed to draw on the behaviour of both the victims and assailants. The problematic effect of such a conclusion was that it failed to equate with some senior officers' investment in the project as, what we deemed to be, a public relations exercise for a 'sinned against' police force. The public relations function was dependent on a sanitised image of the police, which was fundamentally contradicted by accounts which proposed any active, albeit unintended, contribution by the police to the violence committed against them.

Responses to contested meanings

The findings of the research project produced a perspective on assault police which did not accord with that promoted by a number of senior police personnel. While the host police force had strongly supported the research and dedicated a police officer to working on the project, ambivalent responses were received to the conclusions and related recommendations that tackling this particular crime required some attention to police officers' behaviour and attitudes. The line taken by the researchers was that the assailants' behaviour was a given and that organisationally, despite any commitments to youth and community work, the police could have little impact on how individuals behaved. Recommendations emanating from the project, aimed at reducing the force's assault rate and particularly related to conflict management strategies, were therefore targeted at police officers. This approach was interpreted by a minority of senior personnel as an 'anti-police' stance and as being unduly tolerant of the behaviour of those responsible for assaults. Those senior officers who reacted particularly negatively to what they perceived as the blaming of the police, adopted various strategies in an attempt to distance themselves and

72

the force, from the research and its findings. Despite the early commitment to broadening the perspective on assault police to include offenders' accounts, the use of such accounts in practice led to some attempt to marginalise these 'history from below' perspectives and to deny the 'validity' of the findings. This denial applied also to informal and off the record comments by some officers that the approach of some of their colleagues directly contributed to the violence that occurred. Qualitative elements of the research, in particular the shadowing of police officers, identified insider knowledge and understandings that the assertive style of policing adopted by some officers, and in some cases shifts of officers, were linked to higher assault rates in some divisions. However, for organisational purposes, accounts of assault police could only serve functional ends if they depicted the police in a totally positive light, in their eyes, victim-precipitation was not a permissable account, leading them to discredit the whole project. Strategies intended to negate the value of the project included major criticism of the police officer seconded to the project and accusations that he had 'gone native' and failed to protect the image of the organisation. Fundamental criticisms of the research findings also put in question the value of the project as an aid to understanding the dynamics of the problem of assault police and adoption of the pragmatic recommendations included in the report. It proved impossible to challenge the stance and outcomes of the project without setting aside the whole piece. Although off the record, the vast majority of officers agreed that the project had 'got it right' and it was commonplace for officers - like taxi drivers and prison officers we have interviewed - to comment that x is always getting assaulted because of the way he talks to people, the withholding of official approval proved a bar to formally incorporating the recommendations into daily work and training.

Some ten years on, the feedback is that the recommendations of the project are a core element in the training of police officers. Our interpretation is that as the wounds healed, and the personal career interests of those implicitly criticised became irrelevant, the lessons learned from the project were gradually absorbed into the culture of policing and became more in tune with what managers and police trainers are trying to achieve. In the late 1980s, however, while the approach of the media was overwhelmingly supportive of the police, a suggestion from our research that the explanation of police targeted violence lay in the relationship between 'victim' and 'assailant' was perceived as a step too far and as undermining the construction of 'the problem' that had been developed and rendered authoritative by senior police managers.

73

Note

1.   These problems are shared by 'repeat player' researchers, who also risk colonisation and compromise of 'objectivity' in longer-term trade-offs.

References

Amir, M. (1971) *Patterns of Forcible Rape,* University of Chicago Press, Chicago, Ill.

Ditton, J. and Duffy, J. (1983) 'Bias in the Newspaper Reporting of Crime News', *British Journal of Criminology,* 23(2), pp. 159-165.

Elliott, D. and Dowds, L (1989) The 1988 British Crime Survey, *Home Office Research Study No. 111,* HMSO, London.

Ericson, R., Baranek, P. and Chan, J. (1989) *Negotiating Control: a Study of News Sources,* Open University Press, Milton Keynes.

Gatrell, V. (1980) 'The decline of theft in Victorian and Edwardian England' in Gatrell, V., Lenmna, B. and Parker, G. (eds), *Crime and the Law: the Social History of Crime in Western Europe since 1500,* Europa Publications Ltd., London.

Gatrell, V. (1990) 'Crime, Authority, and the Policeman-State, 1750-1950' in Thompson, F. (ed), *The Cambridge Social History of Britain, 1750-1950,* Cambridge University Press, Cambridge.

Hall, S., Critchley, C., Jefferson, T., Clarke, J. and Roberts, B. (1978) *Policing the Crisis,* Macmillan, London.

Home Office (1989) Drinking and Disorder: A Study of Non-Metropolitan Violence, *Home Office Research Study No. 108,* HMSO, London.

Hughes, G (1996) 'The Politics of Criminological Research', in Sapsford, R. (ed) *Researching Crime and Criminal Justice,* Open University (D315 Course Material), Milton Keynes.

Levi, M. (1997) 'Violent Crime', in Maguire, M., Morgan, R. and Reiner, R. (eds) *The Oxford Handbook of Criminology,* Oxford University Press, Oxford.

Pearson, G. (1983), *Hooligan,* Macmillan, London.

Police Review (10 April 1987) '16,000 Officers Assaulted'.

Reiner, R. (1992) *The Politics of the Police,* Wheatsheaf, Brighton.

Reiner, R. (1997a) 'Policing and the Police' in Maguire, M., Morgan, R. and Reiner, R. (eds) *The Oxford Handbook of Criminology,* Oxford University Press, Oxford.

Reiner, R. (1997b) 'Media made criminality: the representation of crime in the mass media', in Maguire, M., Morgan, R. and Reiner, R. (eds)

The Oxford Handbook of Criminology, Oxford University Press, Oxford.

Schlesinger, P. and Tumber, H. (1994) *Reporting Crime,* Clarendon Press, Oxford.

Toch, H. (1969) *Violent Men,* Penguin, Harmondsworth.

5 Accessing a demonised subculture: studying drug use and violence among bodybuilders

Lee Monaghan

> It is not easy to study deviants. Because they are regarded as outsiders by the rest of society and because they themselves tend to regard the rest of the society as outsiders, the student who would discover the facts about deviance has a substantial barrier to climb before he [sic] will be allowed to see the things he needs to see
>
> (Becker, 1963, p. 168).

Introduction

The legality of lifting weights, and the use of certain physique-enhancing drugs (e.g. steroids) in Britain, would appear to render bodybuilding an anomalous inclusion in this edited collection: are bodybuilders really 'deviants' to be brought under the criminological gaze? Although the 1980s fitness boom means that bodybuilding is more mainstream than marginal (Klein, 1993), bodybuilding has long been viewed as a shadowy subculture and a fertile ground for the innuendoes of the amateur psychologist (Thirer and Greer, 1978). Moreover, many of today's 'hard-core' (i.e. dedicated) bodybuilders know (and can articulate upon) the fact that their enterprise is often considered 'suspect' by 'outsiders' (Monaghan, forthcoming). For instance, one bodybuilder whom I interviewed said:

    010: It's still regarded as a subculture in this country I think.
           Like bondage almost! You know, it's like something that's
           done, sort of, you know what I mean? Out of the way!
    LM: It's like, bondage is seen as a bit seedy...
    010: I think a lot of people look on bodybuilders as being like
           that see.
    LM: Honestly?
    010: I think so, yeah. I think so.

The residue of public disrespect hovering over the bodybuilding community (Klein, 1993, p. 248) has recently been exacerbated. The supposed relationship between bodybuilding, steroids and uncontrollable malevolent violence - the so-called 'Roid-Rage' phenomenon publicised by the news media (Dobash *et al.*, forthcoming) - means that muscle enthusiasts have become new 'folk devils' (Cohen, 1980) or 'dangerous individuals' (Foucault, 1988). Correspondingly, bodybuilding - as a 'demonised drug-abusing subculture' - represents a 'closed access group' (Cassell, 1988) for qualitative researchers (cf. Pates and Barry, 1996). This invariably creates problems since fieldwork necessarily entails:

> Subjecting yourself, your own body and your own personality, and your own social situation to the set of contingencies that play upon a set of individuals, so that you can physically and ecologically penetrate their circle of response to their social situation...so that you are close to them while they are responding to what life does to them.
>
> (Goffman, 1989, p. 125)

Referring to my ethnography of bodybuilding, drug use and violence (Monaghan, 1997), this chapter discusses the significance of researcher characteristics when achieving social access i.e. 'getting on' with the researched (Cassell, 1988). Specifically, it highlights the *advantages* of prior participation in the studied culture for the purposes of doing 'face work' (Goffman, 1959), and the benefits of adopting an 'active membership role' (Adler and Adler, 1987); that is, a field role where the ethnographer moves away from the more marginal position of the traditional participant observer. Of course, any 'qualification' for undertaking qualitative research will have both advantages and disadvantages and the reflexive ethnographer must seek to understand all of these (Delamont, 1992; Salisbury, 1994). Exigencies of space, however, mean that this paper only addresses the benefits of prior and active participation alongside some practical difficulties I encountered. First, some background information.

Qualitative work is often based on the researcher's earlier biographical experiences (Alasuutari, 1995; Lofland and Lofland, 1984). Before undertaking ethnographic research on bodybuilding in South Wales - both for a Ph.D. and an Economic and Social Research Council funded project entitled 'Steroids and Violence' (Dobash *et al.*, 1996) - I lifted weights in England for approximately two and a half years (1991 to 1994). Although my prior involvement was largely motivated by a personal interest in sport and exercise, aspects of my biography informed and facilitated systematic social research and the development of ideas broached in a previous study (Monaghan, 1995).

A two year qualitative study was undertaken between 1994 and 1996. After surveying potential sites, overt fieldwork was conducted for sixteen months on a time-sampling basis at several strategic sites. The ethnography was anchored in four hard-core bodybuilding gyms, though research was also conducted elsewhere (e.g. needle exchanges, a Well Steroid User Clinic, a gym in a prison, bodybuilding competitions, night clubs). Participant observation and 67 audio-recorded depth interviews using a semi-structured interview schedule, provided a wealth of qualitative data. Rendered anonymous through the use of pseudonyms (in the case of field notes) and respondent numbers (for interview extracts), these transcribed data were obtained from a range of respondents (both male and female, steroid users and non-users). Data were indexed and prepared for formal analysis, during the last six months of the research project, using coding software; namely, *The Ethnograph* (Seidel, 1988).

Access

Access is often problematic for ethnographers (Hammersley and Atkinson, 1995) and sociologists of 'deviance' (Becker, 1963). It involves establishing and maintaining contact with the researched. Negotiating access typically comprises a physical dimension; namely, getting into the research setting. Particularly powerful or influential individuals ('gate-keepers') may block the researcher's entrance into a setting thus thwarting a study before it commences. Whilst physical access is often a salient consideration for qualitative researchers, the following focuses upon social access. Namely, my ability to *get on* with bodybuilders (many of whom had experience of using steroids), rather than simply getting into bodybuilding gyms.

Before making specific reference to this, the problems of accessing so-called 'deviant' groups are worth emphasising. I would also like to offer a caveat. Cassell (1988) states that for closed access groups (e.g. powerful elites and deviants), discouraging barriers may be erected against those whose presence is perceived to be intrusive. Hence, access is problematic (Cassell, 1988, p. 93 - 95). Although bodybuilding could be considered a closed access group (Pates and Barry, 1996), some important studies have been conducted among steroid-using bodybuilders by non-participants (e.g. Korkia and Stimson, 1993). Thus, in writing this paper I do not wish to contribute to 'insider myths' where it is claimed only members are capable of doing valid research (Hammersley and Atkinson, 1995, p. 109 - 110). Certainly, I am loathe to accept insider doctrines which maintain group members have monopolistic access to new knowledge (Merton, 1972). I am particularly keen to stress this point less the reader should infer that I consider myself an 'Insider as Insighter' (Merton, 1972, p. 15). Given the subject matter of my research, the stigma associated with active or complete membership roles within academia (Adler and Adler, 1987), and the anti-realist critique levelled against much ethnography (Hammersley, 1992), I am *not* presenting myself here as a 'bodybuilder' who is eminently qualified to discover the 'real' or 'true' story. Nevertheless, I would like to emphasise the functions of prior and active participation in the studied group, where social location and the image of the fieldworker, *as held by the respondents*, may facilitate observation and access to particular kinds of knowledge.

Finally, various issues are incumbent upon the reflexive ethnographer when considering social access. For instance, it is possible to think in a detailed and systematic manner about the impact of gender on the fieldwork process (McKeganey and Bloor, 1991; Pettigrew, 1981; Silverman, 1993). Although my research into a male dominated sphere was facilitated by my male gender, prior involvement in gym culture was particularly useful when attempting to 'get on' with group members. Hence I will focus upon the 'achieved' status of prior participant rather than the 'ascribed' gender role.

Social access

Group acceptance and the ability to undertake ethnography among (drug-using) bodybuilders is not automatically conferred through gym membership (i.e. paying a subscription fee to the gym owner). Instead, social access must be achieved through impression management and observing certain rules of action (Goffman, 1959). In the context of the bodybuilding gym this involves, among other things, active participation in weight-training. Exercising with and among the 'natives' meant that I became identifiable as a member in many bodybuilders' eyes. My adoption of an active membership role enabled me to strike-up casual conversations with others and solicit ethnographic data. Achieving social access through direct participation, and talking with other gym members, is highlighted in the following statement made by a competition bodybuilder whom I interviewed:

043: Put it this way, if you were just a college person who comes down the gym who didn't work [train] in the gym and didn't know the people, I bet you'd have totally different answers to what you have got.

For this bodybuilder, 'different answers' meant scant accounts quickly and defensively constructed for non-participants in order to deflect unwanted attention. Accounts intended for non-participants are, of course, sociologically important when researching illicit drug use: they bridge the gap between action and outside expectation (Weinstein, 1980). However, given public disparagement, researchers who are considered 'insiders' by the study population do have a significant advantage in terms of access:

038: All they [outsiders such as journalists] write about is the bad things about bodybuilding and I think the only person who can give you the true facts of bodybuilding is a bodybuilder.

Participating in the gym was helpful in generating positive rapport. This concerns my immediate behaviour, however, rather than being a bodybuilder as such. Observing certain rules of action - namely participation in weight-training - would probably enable any qualitative researcher to access useful information. I was fortunate, however, in that I was already familiar with the intricacies of bodybuilding training. Furthermore, my commitment to training was evidenced in my ability to lift relatively heavy weights. Thus, I could go into a gym and *immediately* be identified as an 'insider' rather than simply a researcher with an interest in the subculture. Because my immediate actions in the gym were shaped by prior participation, I was seen as somebody who was not going suddenly to judge and condemn drug-using bodybuilders. As stated by 043, a bodybuilder who was particularly vocal about the unappreciative attention being focused on the sport at that time:

043: It's like talking to one of their own when they're talking to you. Whereas you bring someone else in, anybody like an outsider, and they will mess people like that around anyway. You know what I mean?

The following exchange similarly highlights the advantages of participating in gyms and being identified as a bodybuilder when achieving social access. Respondent 016 said he would not go to a needle exchange facility (i.e. disclose discrediting information about himself outside the subcultural context) because service providers (non-bodybuilders) would suddenly know his 'secret'. Since I was an academic researcher who was audio-recording his every word, I stated

LM: It's funny how you say like, it's 'your secret'.
016: Within the gym I don't think you mind people knowing so much but I mean it's outsiders who are going to suddenly stereotype you I think is the thing.
LM: Because I train anyway, and I think people talk to me because I'm seen as one of them...
016: Yeah exactly.
LM: But say I was like [just a student] studying this and I wasn't into bodybuilding. Do you think I'd have a harder time getting people to talk to me?
016: Yeah it could be actually. Because you know what I'm talking about. I say something to you, I mean, you can relate to it better.

As noted participant observation would probably enable any qualitative researcher to generate useful ethnographic data. Access to 'sensitive' information, including the indigenous use of ethnopharmacological paradigms, could be obtained through active involvement where the ethnographer becomes 'known to the people' (Etkin, 1993). However, in highlighting how my 'bodybuilder' identity aided social access, 043's comment 'It's like talking to one of their own when they're talking to you' is worth emphasising. Certainly, no suggestion is being made that qualitative methodology entails 'going native' - McKeganey and Bloor (1991), for example, in their discussion of 'The Favourite Uncle', illustrate the usefulness of adopting a field role that *meshes* with the researched when achieving social access. However, prior participation undoubtedly served as a distinct advantage in this study. For instance, I was immediately identified as a bodybuilder by many not simply through action (lifting fairly heavy weights in the gym) but also because of my physical appearance. As a prior participant, aspects of my biography were inscribed on my body, rendering social access relatively unproblematic:

81

(Field-diary extract, 17/5/95: Pumping Iron Gym)

> After interviewing Mike [a drug-using competition bodybuilder
> and national champion] he said something off the tape which is
> relevant to the methodology:
> Mike: 'It [the interview] was good. I liked talking about it.
> Didn't mind at all. It was like talking to a mate really. If
> some skinny guy from the University came into the gym,
> though, asking if he could interview people I don't think I'd
> have done it...'
> Participating, *being seen as a member*, certainly has its
> advantages.

The advantages conferred through prior group membership, and the identity imputed to me by the researched is worth stressing in an ethnography of bodybuilding. This is because a person's presence in the gym, and their participation in training, is not always sufficient in obtaining the bodybuilders' trust. In short, achieving social access, or getting on with bodybuilders, is not a corollary of 'getting in' to the physical context of the gym. As a stratified world, differentiation exists between gym members in terms of, for example, the individual's orientation to lifting weights (not all weight trainers are bodybuilders), physique (muscle is integral in subcultural boundary maintenance), and competition status. Hence, as illustrated below, although bodybuilders are fairly open about their drug use *with other bodybuilders*, they are not necessarily open with people on 'the fringe' (i.e. weight trainers in the gym as opposed to people specifically into bodybuilding):

> 024: I won't tell anybody that I'm taking [steroids], I'll tell
> bodybuilders and I wouldn't like tell, you know, the fringe -
> anyone that come here [to the gym], but anybody that's
> bodybuilding...I'll tell 'em I'm taking.

The same bodybuilder also made the following remark, further highlighting the usefulness of a relative insider identity when achieving social access:

> 024:...it's like you're coming in from the inside you know. You
> imagine if you were just a sociology student or whatever and
> you'd be like probably dumfounded by what you've

82

heard...horrified. And maybe done this report, this research, and not really understood it at the end of the day.

Because those bodybuilders whom I contacted were generally sensitive to mainstream interpretations, the subcultural identity often imputed to me was extremely beneficial in achieving social access. Importantly, access was assisted because I trained as a bodybuilder and - through a history of participation - physically looked more like a 'bodybuilder' than an 'outsider'. Access difficulties encountered by others researching bodybuilding and drug use (e.g. Pates and Barry, 1996) would appear to be minimal for fieldworkers assuming a less marginally involved role and who have been granted indigenous status by the researched. However, I was not always perceived as a group member, especially during the early stages of the research. Furthermore, in conducting an overt study, the 'bodybuilder' identity existed alongside other identities; namely, research student and paid researcher. Difficulties posed by combining different field roles - as they affected social access - are briefly addressed below, alongside how those difficulties were negotiated.

Field roles and social access

Various different theoretical field roles are open to the ethnographer. According to Junker (1960), for example, field roles range from the complete participant to the complete observer. Moreover, such roles are spatially and temporally contingent, varying according to context and at what point the ethnographer is at in their research. Focusing upon the 'bodybuilder' field role which I assumed throughout the main study period, the following teases out and discusses its relation to other, more marginal, field roles which could have compromised social access.

Given some of the practical difficulties and constraints associated with 'complete participation' (e.g. it would be impossible to employ a diverse methodology where interview data are cross-checked with direct observations) I never intentionally concealed my researcher role. Although overt researchers are not constrained to the same degree as those undertaking covert studies to match their personal front with other participants, in achieving access impression management nevertheless remains a salient consideration (Hammersley and Atkinson, 1995, p. 83 - 84). My personal appearance and actions in the generic bodybuilding gym (shaped, as they were, by biography) meant I was not asked continually to account for my presence. Certainly, I had no qualms informing people about my research interests. However, the ease with which I enacted the role of the bodybuilder meant that other gym members did not continually enquire as to why I was there.

During social interaction, and especially upon first meeting people, biographical details were inevitably sought from me. Because I was planning on conducting formally arranged in-depth interviews, I volunteered information about my research interests. However, since the notion of informed consent is often impractical in field research (during transitory encounters immediately stating one's identity as a researcher is disruptive if not destructive of the natural flow of social interaction) I saw no advantage in making it immediately known to everyone that I was a researcher (cf. Bell, 1977; Hornsby-Smith, 1993; Punch, 1986). Indeed, since it is often situationally inappropriate continually to repeat one's research purposes and identify oneself as a researcher (Punch, 1986, p. 37), I tended to volunteer this information in response to other people's questions. Gym members often sought biographical information from me during the early phases of the study; not because they were suspicious, but because I was 'new on the scene' and I did not have a local accent. I responded by divulging information about my research interests.

During research I also obtained receipts from gyms in order to claim expenses from Cardiff University. If gym members wanted to know more about my studies I told them. Although the 'researcher' role could have rendered me an 'intrusive outsider' from the viewpoint of the researched, I believe social access was not compromised. I was confident that my personal commitment to training would negate (or at least minimise) any doubts about my motives. On the most part my confidence was well founded as indicated by the reactions I provoked and as recorded in my field-diary:

(Field-diary extract, 25/5/94: Temple Gym)

After finishing my workout I went to the reception desk to get a receipt (for my expenses), and also a protein drink (so I could 'hang around' for a while). The man behind the counter asked me why I needed a receipt, and I told him I could claim it back from work. Marx [whom I later interviewed] had also just finished his work-out, and he was approaching the desk. The person working there shouted over to Marx that I could claim for my work-outs. Marx was curious so I told him what I was doing...he said: 'Can you get me a job like that?'

84

(Field-diary extract, 18/1/95: Al's Gym)

> I obtained a receipt for my training and told Jabba and Al [the
> gym owners, both of whom I later interviewed] why I wanted a
> receipt. They sounded impressed rather than suspicious that I
> can claim expenses: 'It's good that you can study something
> which is also your hobby.'

Whilst, in general, social access was not compromised by my overt
research interests, several problems did arise because I was simultaneously
involved with an Economic and Social Research Council project explicitly
on steroids and violence. Accounting for steroids and violence is not called
for when bodybuilders engage in routine, commonsense behaviour in a
cultural environment that recognises that behaviour as such (cf. Scott and
Lyman, 1968). Thus, my need to investigate the so-called 'Roid-Rage'
phenomenon prompted some to ask why, as a fellow trainer, I needed to ask
questions on this. I attempted to counter this objection by stating I was
interested in obtaining users' beliefs in order to counter outsiders'
misunderstandings. This, of course, was a partisan statement intended to
reassure drug-using bodybuilders that I did not harbour feelings of
disapproval.

Potential access difficulties, arising through my involvement with the
Economic and Social Research Council project, were generally negotiable.
However, I was informed that some bodybuilders remained suspicious.
Importantly, this occurred after an article was featured in a local newspaper
shortly after commencing research. The article, unfortunately entitled 'Why
Do Steroids Pack a Punch?' (*South Wales Echo* 31/5/94), reported on the
work I was about to undertake as a paid researcher. During the early stages
of the ethnography I attended a bodybuilding competition and discovered
an unfortunate rumour; namely, it was believed that I was a journalist
interested in sensationalising bodybuilding, steroids and violence. This
suspicion, it should be noted, is not unusual in qualitative research: the
accusation of being some type of spy is frequently levelled at ethnographers
(e.g. Aschenbrenner, 1986). One key actor whom I met at this bodybuilding
competition later told me about his suspicions and how he gave me a false
telephone number. One man (whom I call Big Chief), who organised this
physique competition, and a key actor whom I previously contacted
through a formal letter, also alerted me to this whilst I was at the show.

Although I believe I generally overcame these initial misunderstandings
through going to the gym and making myself known, Big Chief told me

nine months after the competition that there were several people at one particular gym who remained suspicious:

(Field-diary extract, 21/3/95: Olympia Gym)

I talked with Big Chief:

LM: 'I remember at the Mr Physique show last year people were coming up to you saying don't speak to me because they thought I was from the papers.'

Chief: 'Some of them are suspicious of you. It's because of this thing about steroids...I suppose with the media taking it all out of context and saying that steroids make you violent. They're gonna be wary.'

The above relates to the question 'what was my field role?' In doing 'face work' (Goffman, 1959) among the researched I presented myself first and foremost as a bodybuilder who also happened to be studying bodybuilding. I may have been an active participant, research student and paid researcher; however, and for the purposes of facilitating social access, I emphasised a personal commitment to bodybuilding and I believe this was my 'master trait' in many gym members' eyes. Consider, for example, the following extract. It illustrates how I negotiated the potential access difficulties arising through combing the field role 'bodybuilder' with 'student', and my ability to 'get on' at a time when bodybuilders were under the scrutiny of an outside gaze:

(Field-diary extract, 5/7/94: Black Gym)

We [Myself and Dan] chatted whilst training. I told him that I was a student undertaking a degree on bodybuilding and steroids. The following exchange occurred:

D: 'So are you a medical student or chemist?'

LM: 'No, sociologist. I'm studying the social side of steroid use and basically talking to users about their experiences whilst on "the gear" [subcultural argot for steroids].'

D: 'Some student came into Thor's Gym last year, last summer it was...he came in wanting to talk to users. He said it was all confidential and everything but the lads just told him to fuck off.'

LM: 'I've not really had that trouble. Most people are quite open about it with me. I think it's because I go to the

gyms to train, you know? I'm into bodybuilding myself. I've also got friends who have taken the gear and it's no big deal.'
[Dan then started to talking about his steroid use.]

Conclusion

Referring to my ethnographic work on a 'demonised' subculture, this chapter has discussed the issue of social access and the significance of field roles and presentation of self. Rejecting so-called 'insider myths', it was accepted that prior and active participation are not prerequisites in ethnographic fieldwork (Hammersley and Atkinson, 1995, p. 91). Researchers without prior involvement in the studied group have demonstrated an ability to conduct ethnopharmacological research in general (Etkin, 1993), and studies of steroid use in particular (Korkia and Stimson, 1993). However, this paper has highlighted how a 'relative' insider identity - imputed to the researcher by the researched and presented by the researcher during fieldwork - might *facilitate* social access. In researching potentially sensitive material, the image which many respondents had of me allowed me, as both researcher and student to obtain particular kinds of knowledge which have so far been omitted from the existing academic literature.

Finally, it should be stressed that disadvantages were also associated with my biography. Although I have discussed possible and probable disadvantages elsewhere (Monaghan, 1997), it is worth reiterating the point that any 'qualification' for undertaking qualitative research will have certain shortcomings (Delamont, 1992; Salisbury, 1994). For example, the researched may rely on shared background expectancies when interacting with the researcher, thus failing to clarify the sense of their everyday remarks (Platt, 1981). Also, the researcher who is somewhat familiar with aspects of the cultural scene may fail in the programmatic task of treating members' practical circumstances as matters of theoretic interest (Delamont, 1996). And, there is the issue of advocacy where the researcher may simply celebrate the studied collectivity without reference to the more 'deviant' aspects of the culture (Silverman, 1993). These methodological issues are clearly significant for those reflexive ethnographers who have moved away from the more marginally involved role of the traditional participant observer.

References

Adler, P.A. and Adler, P. (1987) *Membership Roles in Field Research*, Sage, London.

Alasuutari, P. (1995) *Researching Culture: Qualitative Method and Cultural Studies*, Sage, London.

Aschenbrenner, S. (1986) *Life in a Changing Greek Village*, Dubuque, Kendall/Hunt, Iowa.

Becker, H. (1963) *Outsiders: Studies in the Sociology of Deviance*, Free Press, New York.

Bell, C. (1977) 'Reflections on the Banbury Study', in Bell, C. and Newby, H. (eds) *Doing Sociological Research*, Routledge, London.

Cassell, J. (1988) 'The Relationship of Observer to Observed When Studying Up', in Burgess, R. (ed.) *Studies In Qualitative Methodology*, JAI Press, London.

Cohen, S. (1980) *Folk Devils and Moral Panics: The Creation of the Mods and Rockers*, Martin Robertson, Oxford.

Delamont, S. (1992) *Fieldwork in Educational Settings: Methods, Pitfalls and Perspectives*, Falmer Press, Lewes.

Delamont, S. (1996) 'Familiarity, Masculinity and Qualitative Research', in Carter, K. and Delamont, S. (eds) *Qualitative Research: The Emotional Dimension*, Avebury, Aldershot.

Dobash, R.P, Dobash, R.E. and Bloor, M. (1996) *Steroids and Violence,* Unpublished End of Grant Report, Economic and Social Research Council project: L210252008. Available from the Economic And Social Research Council and authors.

Dobash, R.P., Monaghan, L., Dobash, R.E. and Bloor, M. (forthcoming) 'Bodybuilding, Steroids and Violence: Is there a Connection?', in Carlen, P. and Morgan, R. (eds) *Crime Unlimited: Questions for the 21st Century*, Macmillan, London.

Etkin, N. (1993) 'Anthropological Methods in Ethnopharmacology', *Journal of Ethnopharmacology*, 38, pp. 93-104.

Foucault, M. (1988) 'The Dangerous Individual', in Kritzman, L. (ed) *Michel Foucault: Politics, Philosophy, Culture: Interviews and Other Writings 1977 - 1984*, Routledge, New York.

Goffman, E. (1959) *The Presentation of Self in Everyday Life*, Penguin Books, Middlesex.

Goffman, E. (1989) 'On Fieldwork', *Journal of Contemporary Ethnography*, 18, pp. 123-32.

Hammersley, M. (1992) *What's Wrong With Ethnography?* Routledge, London.

88

Hammersley, M. and Atkinson, P. (1995) *Ethnography: Principles in Practice.* (2ⁿᵈ edition) Routledge, London.

Hornsby-Smith, M. (1993) 'Gaining Access', in Gilbert, N. (ed) *Researching Social Life,* Sage, London.

Klein, A. (1993) *Little Big Men: Bodybuilding Subculture and Gender Construction,* State University of New York Press, Albany, New York.

Korkia, P. and Stimson, G. (1993) *Anabolic Steroid Use In Great Britain: An Exploratory Investigation,* The Centre for Research on Drugs and Health Behaviour, London.

Lofland, J. and Lofland, L. (1984) *Analyzing Social Settings: A Guide to Qualitative Observation and Analysis,* Wadsworth, California.

McKeganey, N. and Bloor, M. (1991) 'Spotting the Invisible Man: The Influence of Male Gender on Fieldwork Relations', *British Journal of Sociology,* 42, pp. 195-210.

Merton, R. (1972) 'Insiders and Outsiders: A Chapter in the Sociology of Knowledge', *American Journal of Sociology.* 78, pp. 9 - 47.

Monaghan, L. (1995) *Becoming A Steroid User: A 'Phenomenological' Approach to the Activity of Steroid Use Amongst Bodybuilders,* Salford Papers in Sociology, 16, Salford.

Monaghan, L. (1997) '*We're Not Druggies, We're Athletes': Bodybuilding, Polypharmacology and Self-Identity* Unpublished Ph.D. thesis, University of Wales, College of Cardiff.

Monaghan, L. (forthcoming) 'Creating "The Perfect Body": A Variable Project', *Body & Society.*

Pates, R. and Barry, C. (1996) *Steroid Use in Cardiff: A Problem for Whom?,* Paper presented to the 7ᵗʰ International Conference on the Reduction of Drug Related Harm, Hobart, Tasmania.

Pettigrew, J. (1981) 'Reminiscences of Fieldwork Among the Sikhs', in Roberts, H. (ed) *Doing Feminist Research,* Routledge, London.

Platt, J. (1981) 'On Interviewing One's Peers', *British Journal of Sociology,* 32, pp. 75-91.

Punch, M. (1986) *The Politics and Ethics of Fieldwork,* Sage, Beverley Hills, California.

Salisbury, J. (1994) *Becoming Qualified: An Ethnography of a Post Experience Teacher Training Course,* Unpublished Ph.D. thesis, University of Wales, College of Cardiff.

Scott, M. and Lyman, S. (1968) 'Accounts', *American Sociological Review,* 33, pp. 46-62.

Seidel, J. (1988) *The Ethnograph: A Users' Guide,* Qualis Research Associates, Littleton co.

Silverman, D. (1993) *Interpreting Qualitative Data: Methods for Analysing Talk, Text and Interaction*, Sage, London.

Thirer, J. and Greer, D. (1978) 'Competitive Bodybuilding: Sport, Art or Exhibitionism?', *Journal of Sport Behaviour*, 1, pp. 186-94.

Weinstein, R. (1980) 'Vocabularies of Motive for Illicit Drug Use: An Application of the Accounts Framework', *The Sociological Quarterly*, 21, pp. 577-93.

6 'Rape from afar': men exposing to women and children

Rosalind Beck

Introduction

Indecent exposure - commonly known as 'flashing' - is typically considered to be a minor sexual offence, as indicated in its status as a summary and not indictable offence. This chapter reports on qualitative research with female victims and discusses the appropriateness of qualitative methods to develop a women's and victims' perspective on an offence where convicted sex offenders have been the key informants to date. It is argued that only by listening to people with experiences of such offences can we develop our understanding of the motivations for such behaviour and the real consequences for victims. This chapter will focus on the rationale for using semi-structured interviews and focus groups and on the substantive findings to illustrate the value of qualitative methods in victim-focused research.

Studies suggest that more than 50 per cent of women have been victims of indecent exposure at some time in their lives (Kelly, 1987; Cox and Maletsky, 1980), and some statistics indicate that it is the most common sexual offence against women (MacDonald, 1973; Radzinowicz, 1957). One estimate is that 40 million women a year are victims of exposing in the USA. In Britain, Kelly (1987) found that half of her sample of 60 women had been victims and McNeill (1982) that 63 per cent of her sample of 100 women had been victimised. The Manchester Survey of Female Victims (1986) found that more women had experienced threatening or obscene telephone calls and indecent exposure than other forms of violence or threatening behaviour. The ease with which victims were found for this study would tend to confirm that it is a very common offence. However a widespread study of prevalence in Britain is yet to be conducted. Indeed, there has been very little recent interest in the subject as reflected in the dates of the publications cited above. The limited recent work on the subject refers to indecent exposure as 'exhibitionism', views it only as a problem for the men who offend, and as an interesting problem for therapists who are concerned with the 'treatment' of these men (Horley,

1995; Rosser and Dwyer, 1996; Miner and Dwyer, 1997).   Indeed, offenders are sometimes portrayed as the victims:

> One third of all sex offences reported to the police are acts of indecent exposure. Yet men who commit this offence *do not always receive the attention they deserve for a problem which may have devastating effects on their personal lives*
>
> (MacDonald, 1973: preface, italics added).

The extent of the problem remains largely hidden, as only a minority of women report the offences to the police (McNeill, 1982). This is true of other violent crime against women. For example, Dobash and Dobash (1992) found that only 2 per cent out of nearly 35,000 violent attacks in their study were reported to the police. Offenders can therefore continue virtually unchallenged by the criminal justice system. This reluctance to report offences is partly explained by the fact that exposing has often not been taken seriously by the police and criminal justice system as a whole. In addition, it has commonly been seen as a legitimate topic for humour. This has also been the case to a certain extent with wife abuse and rape. Actual incidents of exposing are rarely portrayed in popular culture and thus myths about the nature of the offence are perpetuated. The examples of incidents reported below illustrate how a reappraisal of the offence using victims as informants is imperative.

Those who have traditionally presented themselves as having expertise on the subject and who have used offenders as their key informants appear to be bemused by the phenomenon of exposing:

> It is difficult to understand why men rape, plunder and murder, yet these crimes however abhorrent, seem to be more readily explicable than the illegal act of indecent exposure. Many men have fleeting fantasies of forcible sexual relations, robbery and homicide, but thoughts of indecent exposure do not readily spring to mind ... James Bond would not sit in his car waiting to expose himself to a group of school-girls. Much has been written about the origins of exhibitionism, *but still the puzzle remains* (italics added)
>
> (MacDonald, 1981).

Thus using offenders as informants has not been entirely fruitful. Furthermore, exposing has often not been incorporated into feminist analyses of sexual violence and it is argued here that this omission mirrors

92

a societal rejection of it as an issue worthy of serious discussion. Although there has been a heightening of consciousness about obscene telephone calls in the UK in recent years which has resulted in legislation, there has been no comparable action to address the problem of exposing. The research described in this chapter focuses on this neglected topic and is a first step towards putting this problem on the policy agenda. The discussion which follows outlines the methods used and discusses the compatibility of qualitative methods with the priorities of a feminist researcher.

Sampling

The research was conducted in a large Welsh city. There were individual one-to-one interviews (21 with female victims; 4 with male victims) and two focus groups, each comprising of 3 women. The participants were selected on the basis that they had experienced at least one incident of indecent exposure. The ages of the sample at the time of interview ranged from 23 to 57. The reported ages of the victims at the time of the offences ranged from 5 to 55. The estimated ages of the offenders ranged from early teens to early 1990s. The 21 women reported 68 incidents; the four men reported 8 incidents, excluding multiple incidents (for example, within psychiatric hospitals). The incidents occurred between 1945 and 1994. The data on the male victims is reported elsewhere (Beck, 1994) as the focus of this chapter is on women and children as victims.

Snowballing - which is a means of collecting a sample by incremental contacts - was the chosen sampling method. As very few women report incidents of indecent exposure to the police (25 per cent in this study), a sample consisting only of women who had reported the offence would be less representative. Snowballing is conventionally applied to offenders, whereby one burglar, for instance, could give the name of another who may be willing to be interviewed, and so on. In this instance, snowballing was used to obtain a sample of 21 female victims and 4 male victims.

It has been argued that a limitation of snowballing is that one is unlikely to obtain a representative sample. Downes and Rock (1988) have pointed out that one may collect a sample whose politics, stance or milieu are similar to one's own. This certainly happened with my sample. I was working in the mental health field and a disproportionate number of the women had experience of working within that field (7 out of the 21 women). However, it has been argued that in research using focus groups it is necessary for participants to have similar cultural experience as it is

93

this similarity that facilitates the establishment of rapport and makes participants feel free to offer their input (Krueger, 1994). The aim of the study was to chart themes in an unfamiliar and under-researched area. Further quantitative research could look at how representative the experiences reported were.

The use of qualitative methodology and the choice of research subjects

As Cassell and Symon point out:

> there is a high level of expectation that qualitative researchers can and will account for the methodological approach of their work. This is in stark contrast to positivist work, where the legitimacy and relevance of the fundamental method adopted is rarely questioned
>
> (1994, p. 8).

They suggest that if too much time is spent debating the validity of the research design then one courts the danger of being obsessed with the intricacies of the measuring instrument and becoming alienated from the actual behaviour of interest. However, if the research is to be taken seriously its validity must be established.

Small-scale qualitative research on exposing is useful since sexual victimisation has been considerably under-reported in national crime surveys (Stanko, 1988), and surveys have been criticised for other methodological failings (Geis, 1990). Rigid questionnaires set the research agenda in advance and offer no possibility for dialogue, and are thus not the ideal method in exploratory research. It is no longer accepted that in order for research to be deemed 'feminist' it has to be qualitative (Maynard, 1994). Indeed, it been argued that quantitative approaches, if deployed sympathetically, can provide important information on sensitive issues such as sexual abuse (Kelly, Burton and Regan, 1994). However, it was felt that a qualitative approach would yield richer data in this study and was more suited to research which was aimed at developing new perspectives from a group of people not traditionally consulted. The research can be described as feminist in that the participants were treated as experts on their own lives and worthy of respect (Jones, 1994, Radford, 1987, Hanmer and Maynard, 1987). This is a hallmark of feminist research (Maynard and Purvis, 1994).

94

The methodological approach is also one that may enable women to speak easily about what has happened to them, to reflect on their experiences and discuss issues relating to sexual violence in a way that can be positive for them. Many of the women in this study felt that the interviews were akin to counselling sessions. For some it was the first time they had spoken of the incident. It has been argued that there are negative consequences in using these methods, as subjects are asked to focus on painful memories. Holland and Ramazanoglu (1994) have discussed some of the difficulties when researching a sensitive subject and Phoenix (1994) and Kelly, Burton and Regan (1994) have argued against assuming that interviews will be positive experiences for women. Nevertheless, many of the women in this study said that they felt better after the interviews, notably because they felt that they had been taken seriously, often for the first time.

Most research studies to date, with one notable exception (McNeill, 1982; 1987), have used offenders as informants. In offender-based research, convicted men and/or men in psychiatric institutions have been the informants and will not have been representative of the 'typical' offender, if there is such a thing, as the majority of offences go unreported (75 per cent in this study) and only a tiny minority are likely to result in a conviction. Offender-based research may also be unreliable as it may be in the interests of informants to omit certain details of their offences or indeed to deny that they committed them (Scully, 1990).

Victims are a valuable and under-utilised source of information and victim-based research can be a valuable strategy to develop theories about the men's motives for exposing as well as to construct a profile of these men based on women's accounts. Whilst victims of crime are sometimes asked about their perceptions of whether crime has increased or not (Koffman, 1996), for example, it is less common to look systematically at victims' perceptions of the motivations of offenders. Dobash and Dobash (1992) have described how women victims' accounts are marginalised and have advocated moving to a strategy which incorporates their accounts and ends a total reliance on male offenders' perspectives. Women victims will have different views on the offence than offenders and in addition to being able to talk about the consequences for them of having been exposed to, are able to make informed speculations about the offenders' motives. The rationale is that women were there when the offence occurred, they saw the look on the man's face, read his body language and were in a good position to assess the level of threat posed by him.

Often an incident of exposing has been so significant in a woman's life that she has spent a considerable amount of time analysing the possible reasons for the behaviour. Scully (1990) based her study of rapists' motives on offenders' accounts of their behaviour which she then found she had to 'problematise', because they consisted mainly of excuses and justifications. An approach that gives precedence to victims' accounts may be more valid.

The use of focus groups and semi-structured interviews

The focus group technique is generally conceptualised as the use of a semi-structured group session, moderated by a facilitator, held in an informal setting with the purpose of collecting information on a designated topic. A focus group can provide rich details of complex experiences and insight into beliefs and attitudes that underlie behaviour. It is a data collection technique that capitalises on the interaction within a group (Asbury, 1995).

For this study, a semi-structured interview guide was prepared beforehand to help focus the discussion in the interviews and the two focus groups. 21 women were interviewed and 6 women in total took part in the focus groups. It has been suggested that the optimum size of a focus group is 6 to 12 individuals (Asbury, 1995), but I would suggest that when discussing a sensitive topic such as exposing where there is the possibility that participants could become distressed at the recollection of upsetting incidents, that groups of three are satisfactory. In addition, although focus groups are not intended to provide education or emotional support (Carey, 1994), it is helpful if the facilitator has some training in counselling techniques when conducting research on a topic such as sexual victimisation, in order to deal sensitively with the emotions that will invariably become aroused. This is also necessary in order to be able to offer debriefing afterwards. The focus groups were used as a way of extending the data in a group context as well as clarifying some of the data from the interviews. This is an accepted use of the technique (Carey, 1994). A co-facilitator tape-recorded the discussion and made some notes in order to allow the facilitator to focus on the discussion and use effective eye contact with the participants.

Interpreting the data

> As researchers we need to be continuously aware of how problematic interpretation is and will remain. But this does not mean that we are condemned to a feeble, disempowering relativism
>
> (Holland and Ramazanoglu, 1994, p. 143).

96

Interpreting data is thus a methodological challenge. It is a necessary process, however, as work that does not attempt such an interpretation is of limited utility. It has also been argued that it may be counter-productive not to offer interpretations.

> To repeat and describe what women might have to say, while important, can lead to individuation and fragmentation, instead of analysis. Feminism has an obligation to go beyond citing experience in order to make connections which may not be visible from the purely experiential level alone
>
> (Maynard, 1994, p. 23-24).

Holland and Ramazanoglu (1994) advocate a middle way between the extremes of regarding data as reflecting an unproblematic reality and assuming that there is no reality which is knowable through interviews. Thus it is assumed here that there is a reality which can be accessed through people's accounts, but we cannot treat the interpretation as representing some kind of truth.

> The process of interpretation can now be seen as a site of struggle at a critical point of the research, and one on which the presence of the researcher in the research process has a profound effect
>
> (Holland and Ramazanoglu, 1994, p. 131).

From the women's individual accounts, in interview and in the focus groups, it was possible to develop some common themes. Firstly, three victims' accounts are presented in order to contextualise the analysis.

Victims' accounts of incidents

Susan:

> It was the second time I'd been exposed to. I was 34. I witnessed someone masturbating at a window. I suppose I was exposed to - but not necessarily at me personally - it could have been at any woman passing. They target women. This was more significant, more shocking than when it happened when I was a child. In the first incident he was walking along with his willy hanging out; in the second he was masturbating. It was

97

11am on a Monday. I was on my way to the Post Office to get my Family Allowance. He was upstairs in his window - he had a net curtain pulled back so you couldn't see his face. I reacted differently to how I'd expect - I was totally chilled, I went cold. I thought I was broad-minded and unshockable. I got a feeling in the pit of my stomach, like when I found out I was pregnant, like witnessing a car crash. I think he was getting the thrill from seeing my reaction through the net curtain. I have been raped - nothing can frighten me as much as that – but it did shock and frighten me. And I was surprised at other people's reactions - people laughed, made light of it and were almost voyeuristic: 'what was he doing, what did it look like?' The police asked me: 'did he have an erection?'

Janice:

I was 10 at the time - with my cousin, who was the same age. We were cycling up and down a lane. A bloke passed us - he had dark hair, a blue woollen hat and black eyebrows, dressed completely dark. He was about 27 years old and looked like a normal bloke. He had his zip undone and his thing out, and grabbed my cousin and threw her to the ground. I ran – her brother was around the corner but I lost the power of speech - as we were Catholic I couldn't say to a boy the words to describe what was happening. I kept running and went and told my mother. By the time we got back there he had interfered with my cousin and run off. He was caught by the police, because he ran in front of a police car and they were suspicious about him running. I felt pure disgust at myself, because of not being able to speak and disgust with her because she'd been interfered with. I made myself sick because I couldn't sleep with her that night. Her [14 year old] sister said to her 'I hope you washed your hands'. I blamed myself - I thought he'd attacked her because of the way I'd looked at him when he was coming towards us - I was on my big sister's bike, had my head down and was staring at him through my eyebrows as he'd walked into the lane. Even now I feel shame and guilt about leaving her. For years I couldn't talk about it at all. Only in the last few years have I come to terms with it. I never talked to my mother or cousin about it since - it was total taboo. My fear was that he'd kill me and her. I was so scared, I couldn't do anything. I was thinking of myself. I don't get eye contact with men in the street now - I think they're less likely to attack me then.

Mary:

It was the night I decided to leave my husband - and it was the fourth time a man had exposed himself to me. I was 38. I was walking along a road on my way to a friend's house - she was going to put me up for the night. I came to a side road, there were a pile of shrubs on the corner - and out jumped this man, in front of me. He had opened up his zip and was masturbating and he stood there doing it. I thought: 'This is all I need'. I remember thinking I was startled, not afraid. I said: 'For goodness' sake, I don't have time to deal with this, I've got problems of my own. Do yourself up and get some help'. He said: 'Sorry', did himself up and went off. This was about 1.30 in the morning. I was more afraid of my first husband who was very violent, and I felt so relieved to have left him that I felt I could have blown this man over. I felt powerful – that night was the first time I had ever challenged my husband. I felt I could have picked up this little fella and dangled him in my hands.

These accounts illustrate the diversity of women's experiences. Susan's account, for example, demonstrates how the common perception of the impact of exposing is very much at odds with the reality. The fact that friends considered it a humorous event and the police asked questions that the victim considered to be irrelevant, served to trivialise the incident and imply that the victim's reaction to it was not normal. She, too, felt that she had to justify reporting the incident to the police by pointing out to them that the man could also do this in front of children. She said that although she gave the police his address the man was not charged with any offence, as the police said that they 'must catch the man in the act'.

Janice's experience belies the view of these men as harmless, indicating that exposing incidents can be accompanied by hands-on assaults. It further illustrates how, after the event, women and girls can fear that the man will return at a later date. They can be in fear of their lives at the time and after the offence. Incidents can have an enduring impact on later behaviour, with another woman reporting that she would not even go to the shop for a bottle of water after an incident as she felt fearful for her safety outside the home.

The fear of rape and, ultimately, death at the hands of the exposer has been identified in earlier research (McNeill, 1982). Janice's experience also illustrates the tendency of victims to blame themselves for incidents. This is true of women as victims of other crimes, for example, wife abuse (Dobash and Dobash, 1979). Gordon and Riger (1989), in a discussion on victim precipitation pointed out how victims of sexual assault, like so many other victims, tended to look inward to try to locate an explanation for what had happened to them. This is hardly surprising since victims of sexual violence are often blamed by others for their victimisation (Scully, 1990).

Mary's example was quite unusual in that she did not find the incident threatening. As she had been treated violently by her husband for many years, she felt that this was a relatively minor incident. It may also be that the characteristics of the man exposing made him less of a threatening figure than some other men who expose. Each incident of exposing is unique and one must take into account the body language of the man, the location of the incident, the time of day, the presence or absence of other people and other compounding and mitigating factors. One could still not predict the extent to which individual women would be likely to perceive an individual man to be presenting a threat of bodily, as well as psychological, harm to her and in any case such an effort may be of limited utility.

In addition to describing the incidents, women were asked to suggest why the men had exposed to them. There is great value in using victims' expertise on the motivations of offenders as they are able to theorise on possible motives and thus alternative accounts to those which exclusively rely on offenders can be developed.

Motives for exposing

The most basic, yet fundamental feminist question has always been 'why?' Exploring with individuals why they think and act as they do enriches our understanding, and is a far stronger base from which to explore potential change than knowing only what they think and do (Kelly, Burton and Regan, 1994, p.39). Analyses of indecent exposure using offenders as informants have focused on 'external' factors which cause a man to expose - for example, dominant mothers and wives - or factors which free his inhibitions - for example, mental illness and alcohol (MacDonald, 1981). Of the 68 incidents reported in this research, however, mental illness was seen as a likely relevant factor in only two incidents. It was also felt that drink was not a factor. As Scully (1990) has pointed out, there is no biological evidence that drink reduces people's inhibitions, but since there is a societal belief that it does, it enables men to use it as an excuse for their behaviour. One woman in this study felt that the man was acting drunk. She said 'he couldn't have been that drunk because I was walking fast and he was walking alongside and he had no trouble keeping up'.

Typically exposing is not depicted as the individual responsibility of the man who carries out the act. Such work also both over and under-predicts exposing as many men who expose may have no mental health or alcohol problem and men with those problems may not offend. It is not the intention here to offer a critique of such approaches as this has been done elsewhere (McNeill, 1982). Instead, alternative themes based on the accounts of women who have experienced this form of victimisation are presented. It must be acknowledged, however, that the notion of experience is problematic, since individuals do not necessarily possess sufficient knowledge to explain everything about their lives. As Maynard and Purvis (1994) point out

> Accounts will vary depending on such factors as where respondents are socially positioned, memory etc. There is no such thing as 'raw' or authentic experience which is unmediated by interpretation
>
> (Maynard and Purvis, 1994, p. 6).

The women highlighted the functions exposing serves both to the individual men who expose and to men in general. It is not necessary to resort to a crude, conspiratorial model to demonstrate how exposing can be part of a system of social control (Hanmer and Maynard, 1987, p.10). Like other forms of sexual violence exposing is a common and inhibiting feature in women's lives. It can be seen as part of a wider system in terms of its impact on restricting women's freedom, whether the individual exposer is aware of this or not

> It is the family which is the first line of patriarchal power, the state is the last. In-between is the whole range of watching, supervising and controlling of the behaviour of women through the various forms of sexual harassment, abuse and violence
>
> (Radford, 1987, p. 43).

The women often felt that there was a close relationship between the effects the incidents had on them and the motives of the individual man who exposed - for example, that they had been frightened by him and that that had been his intention. Thus one can theorise on the men's motivations by looking at the consequences for women (Beck, 1994). Many of the women were sure that the men had a malicious intent. One said: 'Whether they're disturbed or not, they set out with an intent, I'm quite sure'. Scully has stated with regard to her study of convicted rapists:

> Rather than assuming that rape is dysfunctional behaviour, I use these informants to understand what men who rape gain from their sexually violent behaviour
>
> (1990, p. 59).

Motives identified by the women included:

1. To frighten women

This can be seen within the context of 'fear of crime', which has been identified as a criminological issue since the 1970s as criminologists began to focus on the victim as well as the offender (Zedner, 1997). The results of the British Crime Survey pointed to an apparent irony that fear of crime and victimisation are inversely related and thus, in large part, fear of crime is 'irrational' (Hough and Mayhew, 1985). According to the data it seemed that although men were more likely to be victims of street crime, women expressed more fear of crime. The victimisation of women through wife abuse, rape, sexual harassment and so on, was greatly under-represented particularly in the data gathered from early sweeps of the survey. Since then a considerable amount of feminist research has been conducted on fear of sexual assault which has gone some way towards redressing the allegations of irrational responses by women (Kelly, 1988; Hanmer, Radford and Stanko, 1989).

The women perceived that a central aim of the exposer was to frighten women in general and children. Scully found that rapists 'both perceived and enjoyed the fear they evoked in victims' (1990, p.137). One prisoner at Grendon convicted of rape said: 'the more fright I could see in her eyes, the more I got a kick out of it' (quoted in Teague, 1993, p. 38). Similarly, a woman in the current study on being asked 'why do you think he did it? [i.e. exposed to her]' said, simply: 'to see the fear in my face'. Men who exposed were in effect frightening the woman with the threat of further (hands-on) assault against her. Few of the women considered that they were individually targeted and it was felt that the selection of the victim was often opportunist and arbitrary.

102

It was not necessary to have experienced incidents directly to be affected by them. In this study, one woman (Patricia) was affected by an incident that her sister experienced. Her sister was in the local pub, which was very busy at the time, went to the toilets and was sitting on the toilet when a man pushed open the door (which had no lock) and masturbated in front of her. After this Patricia was too frightened to go to the toilet alone in pubs, and this made me, as the researcher, also wary. This is a hazard for the researcher on sexual violence, who can become 'overwhelmed by an awareness of male violence' (Kelly, 1988, p.15). It is important that researchers are not only aware of the effects of research on the respondents but also on them as researchers (Stanley and Wise, 1993), and indeed on the people who read the research. Thus exposers can frighten not only their immediate victim but women in general.

2. *To shock and surprise women*

'I didn't say anything when he did it. I can't believe it – I wish I'd not been such a wimp. I'm annoyed about that' (Eve)...'But don't you think that's part of it? Don't you think they know that, that you're not going to be able to say anything?' (Catrin)... 'Probably' (Eve)... 'They often target a woman alone'

(Karen) (transcribed from focus group discussion).

An intention of the exposer could be to make a woman feel 'stupid' for not having the time, ability or courage to react assertively. The surprise element is crucial here, and is of course a central feature of exposing. Women can feel powerless at the time of the incident. They are unable to predict, and thus unable to control, men's behaviour or anticipate when it might lead to violence (McNeill, 1987).

3. *To exercise power over women*

In both Britain and the USA, radical feminists since the 1970s have focused on the violation of women's bodies as the site of oppression (Brownmiller, 1975, Daly, 1979; Dworkin, 1974), and power has been seen as a central motivation of men who are sexually violent towards women. The women in this study felt that there was an inherent threat in the act of exposing. When men expose to women they play upon the demonology of stranger attacks, which would suggest that they are likely to physically assault the woman. The exercise of this power over women was seen as a central motive in exposing, and was mentioned by many of the women. For example,

> They get a lot of power over you...it's humiliating...you're not sure what they're actually going to do - masturbate, or take it further and assault you - so you feel powerless and the fact that you're surrounded by people and that that person feels safe enough to do it, and knowing that nobody's going to intervene, that gives him a different sort of power over the other people - he's got so much attention and control over everyone'.

Another woman said 'I felt much more the power and control thing - you will serve my purposes - and I'll always remember how he walked off with a smile on his face'.

4.   To threaten rape and murder

The women felt an aim of exposing was to serve as a reminder to women that they may be raped. McNeill found evidence that incidents of exposing 'served to *remind* women of the threat [of rape and death]' (italics in the original). This was confirmed in this research

> I was with my friend - we were both 17 - it was about 1am. He said 'No, I want you', and pointed at me. I screamed – she couldn't - she was in real shock and she ran. He said I should sit and watch him and then he wouldn't hurt me, but that if I ran, he'd come after me. I felt complete terror - I thought 'this is the end'.

Daly (1979) felt that the 'possession of women's minds' is more significant than physical intimidation. She saw 'mind-rape' as more powerful than 'body-rape'. Similarly, obscene phone calls have been described as 'mental rape' (Wyre and Swift, 1990) and some women consider them to be as serious as physical rape. This theme was repeated by the women in this study, one of whom felt exposers 'try to get into your head' (Karen), as well as being physically intimidating. But, of course, all sexual assaults affect women's minds as well as bodies. One woman who had been raped and exposed to in separate incidents said:

There is a link with rape - with the violent act of rape, the pleasure out of seeing women shocked and struggling to get an erection....[Exposing] is like rape from afar.

5. *Other motives*

Some women felt that men who expose try to enforce social control over women. This is a common theme in explanations of violent acts (Hanmer and Maynard, 1987). For example, as with rape, women can restrict their lives after they have been exposed to, and more than one woman felt this was the intention of the exposer. A couple of the women felt that the exposer was attention-seeking. Another felt that exposers could use a woman as a representation of his fantasy. This is confirmed in studies of offenders. It has been claimed that exposing is 'merely an enactment in daily life of his fantasies in dreams' (MacDonald, 1973). At least two women suggested that men may expose to try to combat impotency.

One woman in a focus group felt that: 'People make choices and perhaps the man has chosen to expose himself rather than do something else, which may be worse' (Mary). Hence, she saw exposing as catharsis. Another woman in the group felt that it had the opposite effect: 'I tend to think the more you do it, the more you want to' (Rhiannon). One woman was exposed to by a man on one occasion and then some time later was exposed to and indecently assaulted by the same man (Kate). This could perhaps be viewed as two points in his 'career' of sexual offending.

6. *Benefits to other men*

Whilst individual men who expose may not see themselves as enforcing social control over women on behalf of other men, the women suggested ways it could benefit other men, and thus these can also be conceptualised as (subconscious) motives.

It's violence against women, an invasion, an intrusion, it has the result of making women feel guilty - What have I done wrong? I shouldn't have been there...and terrorising us and putting us in our place...And making us not want to walk out at night, or walk alone in the woods or across the park
(focus group discussion).

Thus, it may be in the interests of many men to have the exclusive use of public spaces. Another woman pointed out

105

It gives them a scapegoat for things they might like to do themselves - men get a topic for jokes. I think a lot of men look at women in the street and get an erection. So, with someone going a step further than that, they are all doing it, in a private way. And they belittle it quite a lot.

Some women felt that men benefited in the role of spectator. In reference to an incident on the London tube where men looked on and did nothing

Maybe they were getting off on it. She was an attractive woman. It was like entertainment for them, the way they were so passive. Like some sort of show, they were maybe curious about what would happen next. It shocked me - I expected one of them to help her, but none did.

It was further felt that male partners could revel in the role of rescuer or protector. McNeill (1982) found that one benefit to other men is that women become more subservient to men they know as a result of such incidents, for example, sexually. One woman interviewed said

It empowers men - women are the victims, then men see themselves as the rescuers...they get more control over you... They might also say: 'What were you wearing?' especially if you have a partner who doesn't like the way you dress...he can then also control what you wear...and he could say 'you shouldn't go out at night'.

More than one woman made reference to a partner being able to control what she wore as a result of being exposed to

Of course it makes him feel great [the boyfriend/husband], he's in control, he's controlling you - he can say: 'You can't walk home alone, remember what happened'...and it makes them look good: 'Aren't there some perverts about? I'd never do that'.

Another woman had no doubt about this:

It would have played right into the hands of all my previous partners and current one - because it would give him the excuse he needed either to prevent me doing anything on my own, or to take me places, meet me, control me - and that would apply to each one of them [three partners].

Conclusion

Often, a research project is deemed to have finished when the researcher has written up their interpretation of the data. Rarely are participants given the opportunity to remark on the researcher's interpretation. The women in this study were offered this opportunity informally and six women expressed an interest in reading the completed thesis and commenting on it. Although they did not provide critical comments on specific issues in it, several stated that it was useful to see the whole picture as they had previously seen their own experience as unique. One woman said that it made her rethink the way in which she had allowed herself to be a victim in her life and as a result of reading the thesis, she took legal action against her neighbour who had been sexually harassing her over the telephone, calling her obscene names in the garden and had been a 'Peeping Tom' for over twenty years. Focus group participants also had this opportunity of seeing the broader picture by sharing their experiences with others. Having the participants review the analysis can also serve the function of checking the validity of the researcher's interpretation (Maynard and Purvis, 1994). Such research practice can be seen as an ethical imperative in feminist research (Maynard and Purvis, 1994). As I conducted this research as part of a self-financed, part-time Masters Degree, while working full-time in a completely different field, time constraints prevented me from the ideal of incorporating their interpretations into the final version.

The substantive findings can be summarised as follows: exposing is one expression of sexual aggression against women. Nevertheless, it is an offence which is often omitted in research using the concept of a continuum of sexual violence. This omission implies that it is a minor offence not worthy of attention. The women in this study have shown how being a victim of this form of sexual attack can have a significant impact on their lives and can be interpreted by them as a message from the man that if he chose to he could also rape or murder them. As the incidents often happen when the woman or child is alone in an isolated place this is experienced by them as a very real threat. These facts about exposing are hidden behind a mythology of the stereotypical harmless 'flasher' who will do 'nothing else' to the victim, and who provides a topic for jokes and humour. This also perpetuates an unhelpful police response to the victims (Hanmer and

Maynard, 1987). Exposing is, therefore, not a minor and 'non-violent' crime against women and there needs to be a considerable amount of re-interpretation of it so that victims are taken seriously in the future.

References

Asbury, J.E. (1995) 'Overview of focus group research', *Qualitative Health Research*, 5, 4, November 1995, pp. 414-420, Sage, Thousand Oaks, CA.

Beck, R.D. (1994) *'Rape from Afar': Men Exposing Themselves to Women and Children*, Unpublished MSc (Econ.) thesis, University of Wales, Cardiff.

Brownmiller, S. (1975) *Against Our Will*, Penguin, Harmondsworth.

Carey, M.A. (1994) 'The group effect in focus groups: planning, implementing and interpreting focus group research', in Morse, J. (ed) *Critical Issues in Qualitative Methodology Research*, Sage, Thousand Oaks, CA.

Cassell, C. and Symon, G. (1994) *Qualitative Methods in Organisational Research: A Practical Guide*, Sage, London.

Cox, D. and Maletsky, B. (1980) 'Victims of exhibitionism', in Cox, D.J. and Daitzman, R.J. (eds), *Exhibitionism*, Garland, New York.

Daly, M. (1979) *Gyn-Ecology: The Meta-Ethics of Radical Feminism*, Women's Press, London.

Dobash, R Emerson and Dobash, R.P.(1992) *Women, Violence and Social Change*, Routledge, London and New York.

Dobash, R Emerson and Dobash, R.P (1970) *Violence Against Wives*, The Free Press, and Macmillan Distributing, Basingstoke.

Downes, D. and Rock, P. (1988) *Understanding Deviance*, Clarendon Press, Oxford.

Dworkin, A. (1974) *Woman Hating*, E.P. Dutton, New York.

Geis, G.(1990) 'Crime Victims: Practices and Prospects', in Lurigio, A.J., Skogan, W.G. and Davis, R.C. (eds) *Victims of Crime: Problems, Policies and Programs*, Sage, Newbury Park, California.

Gordon, M.T. and Riger, S. (1989) *The Female Fear*, Free Press, New York.

Hanmer, J., Radford, J. and Stanko, E.A. (1989) *Women, Policing and Male Violence*, Routledge, London.

Hanmer, J. and Maynard, M. (1987) *Women, Violence and Social Control*, MacMillan, London.

Holland, J and Ramazanoglu, C (1994) 'Coming to Conclusions: Power and Interpretation in Researching Young Women's Sexuality', in Maynard, M. and Purvis, J. (eds) *Researching Women's Lives from a Feminist Perspective,* Taylor and Francis, London.

Horley, J. (1995) 'Cognitive-behavioural Therapy with an Incarcerated Exhibitionist', *International Journal of Offender Therapy and Comparative Criminology,* 39 (4), pp. 335-339.

Hough, M. and Mayhew, P. (1985) *Taking Account of Crime: Key Findings from the 1984 British Crime Survey,* Research Study, 85, HMSO, London.

Jones, E. (13 September, 1994) Workshop on Child Sexual Abuse at Sully Hospital, South Glamorgan.

Kelly, L., Burton, S. and Regan, L. (1994) 'Researching Women's Lives or Studying Women's Oppression? Reflections on What Constitutes Feminist Research' in Maynard, M. and Purvis, J. (eds) *Researching Women's Lives from a Feminist Perspective,* Taylor and Francis, London.

Kelly, L. (1987) 'The Continuum of Sexual Violence' in Hanmer, J. and Maynard, M. (eds) *Women, Violence and Social Control,* MacMillan, London.

Kelly, L. (1988) *Surviving Sexual Violence,* Polity Press, Cambridge.

Koffman, L. (1996) *Crime Surveys and Victims of Crime,* University of Wales Press, Cardiff.

Krueger, R.A. (1994) *Focus Groups: A Practical Guide for Applied Research,* Sage, Thousand Oaks, CA.

MacDonald, J.M. (1981) 'Sexual Deviance: the Adult Offender', in Mrazek, P.B. and Kempe, C.H. (eds), *Sexually Abused Children and their Families,* Pergamon Press, Oxford, pp. 89-94.

MacDonald, J.M. (1973) *Indecent Exposure*: Preface, III, Charles C. Thomas, Springfield.

McNeill, S. (1982) *Flashing - Its Effect on Women,* M.A.Dissertation, Dept. of Social Administration, University of York.

McNeill, S. (1987) 'Flashing: Its Effect on Women' in Hanmer, J. and Maynard, M. (1987), *Women, Violence and Social Control,* MacMillan, London.

Manchester Survey of Female Victims (1986), reported in *Police Watch* (July, 1987).

Maynard, M. and Purvis, J (1994) 'Doing Feminist Research', in Maynard, M. and Purvis, J. (eds) *Researching Women's Lives from a Feminist Perspective,* Taylor and Francis, London.

Miner, M.H. and Dwyer, S.M. (1997) 'The Psychosocial Development of Sex Offenders: Differences Between Exhibitionists, Child Molesters and Incest Offenders', *International Journal of Offender Therapy and Comparative Criminology*, 41 (1), pp. 36-44.

Morgan, D.L. (1988) *Focus Groups as Qualitative Research*, Sage, Newbury Park, CA.

Phoenix, A (1994) 'Practising Feminist Research: The Intersection of Gender and 'Race' in the Research Process', in Maynard, M. and Purvis, J. (eds) *Researching Women's Lives from a Feminist Perspective*, Taylor and Francis, London.

Purvis, J. (1994) 'Doing Feminist Women's History: Researching the Lives of Women in the Suffragette Movement in Edwardian England' in Maynard, M. and Purvis, J. (eds) *Researching Women's Lives from a Feminist Perspective*, Taylor and Francis, London.

Radford, J. (1987) 'Policing Male Violence - Policing Women', in Hanmer and Maynard, (1987) *Women, Violence and Social Control*, MacMillan, London.

Radzinowicz, L. (1957) *Sexual Offences: Report of the Cambridge Department of Criminal Science*, MacMillan and Co., London.

Rosser, B.R.S. and Dwyer, S.M. (1996) 'Assessment, Psychosexual Profiling and Treatment of Exhibitionists', *Journal of Offender Rehabilitation*, 23 (3-4), pp. 103-123.

Scully, D. (1990) *Understanding Sexual Violence: A Study of Convicted Rapists*, Harper Collins Academic, London.

Stanko, E.A. (1988) 'Hidden Violence Against Women', in Maguire, M. and Pointing, J. (eds) *Victims of Crime: A New Deal?* Open University Press, Milton Keynes and Philadelphia, pp. 40-46.

Stanley, L. and Wise, S. (1993) *Breaking Out Again*, Routledge, London.

Teague, M. (1993) *Rapists Talking About Rape*, Social Work Monographs, Norwich.

Wyre, R. and Swift, A. (1990) *Women, Men and Rape*, Hodder and Stoughton, London.

Zedner, L. (1997) 'Victims', in Maguire, M., Morgan, R. and Reiner, R. (eds) *The Oxford Handbook of Criminology*, Oxford University Press, Oxford.

Part two:
Responses to crime and criminal activity

7   Researching women awaiting trial: dilemmas of feminist ethnography

Emma Wincup

Introduction

A willingness to talk openly, and at length, about the process of conducting research, has been a particular feature of qualitative social science in recent years. In part, this can be attributed to the influence of feminist researchers who have demonstrated a concern with recording the subjective experiences of conducting research (Maynard and Purvis, 1994; Roberts, 1981). This chapter follows in this tradition and reflects upon my experiences of conducting ethnographic research with women awaiting trial which was informed by a feminist perspective. It documents the natural history of a research project from the initial stages of the research design through to the production of the final ethnographic account. The settings in which this took place include three bail hostels (Carlton House, North Street Hostel and Victoria House - all pseudonyms) and one remand centre. With the exception of North Street Hostel which was a hostel for both female and male bailees, the settings only accommodated women.

Designing a feminist research project

The notion of an exclusive feminist method has been challenged by researchers working inside and outside the feminist tradition. Many feminist researchers have argued against the existence of an exclusive feminist method. Feminist researchers do not have a blueprint to follow when designing their research projects (Gelsthorpe and Morris, 1990). Rather as Kelly (1990) argues, they need to develop methodologies appropriate to the research questions(s) and avoid methodological purism. The issue then becomes how to apply a feminist perspective to the research method(s) employed. In spite of this, a number of key themes within feminist research projects can be delineated. Gelsthorpe (1990) suggests three common themes: first, choosing topics which are relevant or sympathetic to women and to the women's movement; second, a preference but not an exclusive focus on qualitative research; and third, a reflexive approach, particularly to issues of power and control and a concern to record the subjective experiences of doing research. Drawing on these themes, the research project on which this chapter is based can be regarded as an example of feminist research.

Feminist critiques of academic disciplines have been influential in reorienting research agendas towards topics which are relevant to women's lives. Within criminology, a 'patchwork' (Heidensohn, 1994) of knowledge has been developed by feminist criminologists on the experiences of female offenders and their treatment within the criminal justice system. Inevitably there are gaps within this knowledge. The experiences of women awaiting trial, and the criminal justice response to these women, is an example of such a gap. Many feminist research projects originate from women's experiences. For some researchers these are direct experiences; for example, Roseneil's (1993) research on the Women's Peace Camp at Greenham Common where she was living at the time. In the case of the research reported in this chapter, they are indirect experiences. Whilst studying courses on imprisonment, I began to read a number of autobiographical, highly critical accounts of women's imprisonment (Carlen, 1985; Padel and Stevenson, 1988; Peckham, 1985). One in particular held my attention: Audrey Peckham's account of her time awaiting trial. Her descriptions of the humiliations and degradations of waiting anxiously for trial in a remand centre where she was denied access to appropriate psychiatric care were disturbing, particularly her suggestion that her treatment on remand was worse than her treatment as a convicted, sentenced prisoner.

Peckham's account concluded with a suggestion that, where possible, defendants should be diverted from the remand system to supportive institutions such as bail hostels. Unsure about the role of bail hostels in the criminal justice system, but having read similar suggestions by penal pressure groups and academic criminologists, I selected the study of bail hostels as an alternative to women's imprisonment as my research topic. More specifically, the research aimed to answer two questions: first, what are the particular problems experienced by women awaiting trial? and secondly, how do bail hostels aim to offer support and what are the factors which facilitate or impinge upon the provision of support? The concern with women awaiting trial needs further exploration. As Carlen (1994) argues, it is potentially problematic to focus exclusively on sexism and the social regulation of women without examining the specifics of the state punishment of offenders. Regarding the power to punish as a means to oppress women and men 'independently of the gender specific modes wherein it is activated' (p.137), she argues that 'the study of women's and men's imprisonment could be usefully federated to constitute a more focused analysis of penality' (p.138) which challenges the power to punish. The decision to focus on women awaiting trial is guided by personal interest and practical constraints, rather than a desire to keep feminist research 'on, by and for' women. As an exploratory study, the research takes as its starting point the experiences of women awaiting trial.

Having selected the research topic and an appropriate theoretical framework (what could be loosely termed a 'feminist criminological' perspective), the next stage was to determine what methods could help me to understand women's experiences. ¹A qualitative approach appeared to be the most appropriate, whereby rich and detailed data could be collected and presented to a future audience through meaningful analytic descriptions of how social life is accomplished. Unlike the position adopted by earlier feminist researchers such as Graham (1984), the choice of qualitative techniques is not based on the premise that only qualitative approaches can be used to generate the kinds of knowledge that feminists wish to develop, and that only qualitative approaches are compatible with the politics of feminism. This viewpoint developed from a critique of quantitative approaches which were seen to represent 'masculinist' forms of knowledge, emphasising objectivity and the detachment of the researcher. I do not hold this view. As others have also noted (Kelly, 1990; Kelly et al, 1992; Pugh, 1990), research involving quantification has made an important contribution to our knowledge and understanding of women's lives; for example, through raising awareness of the nature and extent of violence against women. The choice of a qualitative approach is based on the apparent appropriateness to an exploratory study which had an emphasis on investigating the subjective experiences and meanings of those who live and work in remand centres and bail hostels. Marshall and Rossman (1989, p.46) confirm this congruence between the aims of the research and a qualitative approach:

> The strengths of qualitative studies should be demonstrated for research which is exploratory or descriptive and that stresses the importance of context, setting and subject's frame of reference.

Feminist researchers do not simply utilise pre-existing research techniques, rather they adapt them to mesh with their gender-conscious theoretical position. Whilst feminist researchers have appreciated the compatibility between qualitative semi-structured approaches to interviewing and feminist concerns, they have been highly critical about the ways in which traditional textbook guidelines constrain researchers (Finch, 1984; Oakley, 1981). In these, the interview is seen as a hierarchical relationship between the researcher and the 'researched' in which rapport is established as a means to gain richer data and emotional attachment should be avoided at all costs. Instead, feminists advocate a less exploitative relationship based on informality, equality, sharing information, empathy, genuine rapport and subjectivity.

There is now recognition that some of the earlier ideals of feminist research are difficult to establish in practice. For instance, the view that research can be based on non-hierarchical relationships has been challenged in the light of recent feminist debates which have questioned the essentialist foundations of feminism and drawn our attention to differences which divide women, particularly the divisions of ethnicity, class, age and sexuality (Anthias and Yuval-Davis, 1983; Hill Collins, 1990; Spelman, 1990). This has filtered through to feminist criminology (Rice, 1990; Smart, 1990). Consequently, the debate has moved on from an uncritical acceptance that a methodological approach can be adopted which is fully congruent with feminist concerns, to a stance which argues for the need to consider the potentials and dilemmas of methods used in feminist research. In this vein, the chapter now considers why an ethnographic approach was adopted and highlights issues which arose from my own research about the compatibility of ethnography with feminist perspectives.

Why ethnography?

An ethnographic approach was adopted to allow empathic understanding of criminal justice institutions for women (remand centres and bail hostels) and the lives of women who live and work in them. Within criminology, the ethnographic tradition has been long established to study criminal groups such as drug users (Becker, 1963), gangs (Thrasher, 1927) and working class villains and entrepreneurs (Hobbs, 1988). Indeed, some researchers have suggested that ethnography has been especially reliant on studies of deviance (Adler and Adler, 1995; Lofland, 1987; Manning, 1987). More recently, ethnographic approaches have been used to explore the workings of the criminal justice system (Eaton, 1986; May, 1991; Rock, 1993).

The essential characteristics of ethnography include involvement in people's lives for an extended period of time, watching what happens, listening to what is said, asking questions. This takes place within their 'natural' setting. These characteristics resemble the ways in which people make sense of their everyday lives, and this has been regarded as a fundamental strength of ethnography for some social scientists (Hammersley and Atkinson 1995). Reflecting on her own research on young women and further education, Skeggs (1994) suggests that ethnography is a theory of the research process which provides interpretation and explanation through strategies of contextualization. It is a methodology which involves certain features in specific ways rather than a research method. Consequently, there is potential to mix methods and contemporary ethnography tends to be multi-method research combining participant observation, interviews and documentary analysis (Pearson, 1993; Reinharz, 1992).

In combining methods, ethnographers are not suggesting naively that mixing methods will increase the validity of their data or that the data gathered from different sources can be used to produce a single unitary picture of the 'truth'. Both feminists and ethnographers have criticised this simplistic view. Postmodern analysis has been influential here. The core element of feminist postmodernism is the rejection of one unitary reality through recognising differences between women and thus the demise of total explanations of oppression. Feminist research is no longer seen as a means to establish feminist truth and objective knowledge but is concerned with 'the deconstruction of truth and analysis of power effects which claims to truth entail' (Smart, 1990; p.82). Research by feminists uncovers subjugated knowledges and multiple versions of reality.

The insights of postmodernism have also impacted upon debates about ethnography. The realist notion that the researcher can 'tell it how it is' and can write ethnographic accounts which present social reality in an unproblematic manner has come under attack as postmodern analyses have encouraged reflexivity and challenged traditional modes of representation (Coffey and Atkinson, 1996; Denzin, 1997; Marcus and Fischer, 1986; Clifford and Marcus, 1986). The inherently political nature of the research process and the construction of ethnographic texts has been brought to the fore, and issues such as language, the nature of representation and power relations dominate current debates (Atkinson 1990, 1992). It therefore appears that feminism and ethnographic practice have shared concerns. However, the compatibility between the two must not be taken for granted.

Dilemmas of feminist ethnography

The relationship between feminism and ethnography has been explored by a number of feminist researchers (Clough, 1992; Olesen, 1994; Reinharz, 1992; Stacey, 1988; Wolf, 1992). Of particular concern is Judith Stacey's (1988) claim that feminist ethnography is fundamentally contradictory. She suggests that feminist scholars have identified ethnographic methods as ideally suited to feminist research because of their contextual, experiential approach to knowledge emphasising empathy and human concern, and because they facilitate equal and reciprocal relationships between knower and known. However, Stacey argues that paradoxically such methods subject research participants to greater risk of exploitation, betrayal and abandonment than in positivist research. Her concerns lie with the research process and its product. Fieldwork, she points out, inevitably represents an intrusion, an intervention into a system of relationships that the researcher can leave more freely. Moreover, there are difficult compromises to be made between respect for participants and producing an authentic account when research participants are promised control over the final product. Despite this, she believes the potential benefits of a 'partially' feminist ethnography seem worth the serious moral costs involved.

This view is not shared by all. Instead, many feminist researchers have drawn our attention to the dilemmas of feminist ethnography, yet at the same time do not regard feminist ethnography as a contradiction in terms. For example, whilst acknowledging the potential of feminist ethnography to make women's lives visible, Reinharz (1992, p.65) notes that 'feminist ethnography is burdened with many controversies and dilemmas'. She labels these the problem of trust, the closeness/distance dilemma and the dilemma of the complete participant/complete observer. The problem of trust refers to the realisation that rapport and trust are not immediately established on the basis of some shared sisterhood. Instead, this must be worked at. A further dilemma is that the development of closeness to further understanding may be seen as 'going native' or over-rapport. This is problematic in two ways in that it might be seen to compromise the very academic understanding that feminist ethnographers set out to achieve, but it can also be seen as exploitative in the sense that superficial friendships are created for the purpose of data collection. Total immersion in the social world in which they are studying through complete participation in it as a member of that social world can be seen to comprise their very academic understanding of it. Such participation is viewed positively by some feminist researchers as a means of integrating their selves into their work and eliminating the distinction between subject and object (Roseneil, 1993; Stanley and Wise, 1993).

These dilemmas cannot be easily resolved and they shatter any images of ethnography as simple. What the critiques elude to, a point that Hammersley and Atkinson (1995) make explicitly, is the need for reflexivity. Within the ethnographic traditions, calls for reflexivity have been made strongly (Hammersley and Atkinson, 1995). What follows is a discussion which documents my experiences of conducting ethnographic research, in particular highlighting the potential dilemmas of feminist ethnography for researching women awaiting trial.

Reflections on the research process

Other researchers have commented on their early days in the field (Geer, 1964; Van Mannen, 1991). From my own experience, they were anxious times. I had little experience of working in criminal justice agencies and no contact with female offenders until I began the research. I felt uneasy in an unfamiliar setting. I felt apprehensive being surrounded by individuals charged in some cases of very serious offences. This stemmed not from fear of victimisation rather from my inability to predict how the women would react to an outsider conducting research on their lives. They might consider my presence to be a intrusion of their privacy. This is heightened when conducting research in a criminal justice institution. Women within them are often distrustful of others, sometimes a product of previous life experiences such as violence and abuse. Whilst I was conscious to gain their consent, when conducting ethnographic research this is problematic. There is the potential for individuals, even if they are not directly involved, to be 'sucked in' unwittingly. The constraints on their liberty especially in the prison made it difficult for them to walk away. In practice, the women were generally positive towards me and welcomed the interest of another in their lives. However, a relationship based on trust and rapport needed to be established and could not be taken for granted on the basis of shared sisterhood. The women hostel residents and prisoners I met were a diverse group but often there were differences of class, lifestyle and in some cases age, ethnicity and sexual identity between the women and myself. For this research project, the very fact that the women were charged with a criminal offence and were experiencing restrictions on their liberty, to varying extents, created a further barrier.

One of the most difficult aspects was trying to establish a role. Working in a number of settings makes it difficult to generalise about my role, but some general assumptions can be made. In all settings I was a researcher, yet I sometimes took on additional roles in different settings. Within the prison, I was a teacher, a volunteer and a student. Within hostels, I was also seen as a student, a visitor and someone to talk to. Fitting my role as a researcher into the ideal types proposed by Schwartz and Schwartz (1955) and Gold (1958), I adopted an active participant-as-observer role. In some ways this was dictated to me by the research settings and the research participants. For example, within the prison, I was constantly asked to help with class work or computing instruction or to participate in discussion groups. Deep suspicion was shown about visitors who adopted what they termed a 'zoological' approach, looking at but not talking to the women. I found the role of complete observer potentially exploitative.

At times though, particular roles were assigned to me. I was often mistaken within the prison for an inmate, illustrating the powerful influence of stereotypes. I was seen as too young to be a researcher and since most female prisoners are young, the assumption was made that I was an inmate. Consequently, I was almost locked in a cell, almost searched by prison officers and offered counselling by a volunteer from the Salvation Army! The women on remand rarely made this assumption. Dressed smartly (an attempt to avoid being mistaken for an inmate and therefore searched or locked in a cell) and ignorant of some of the prison jargon, I was not one of them. The problem of mistaken identity happened within the hostels too. I was frequently mistaken in the early stages for a staff member, a relief worker, or a social worker. In part, this is an attempt to make sense of my presence within a criminal justice institution. The women hostel residents and prisoners saw me as an interested individual yet were intrigued as to why I would choose to spend long periods of time in a criminal institution.

Unlike other criminological researchers, I was not treated with any real suspicion. Researchers in prison settings have commented on how they were designated as spies (Carter, 1995; Sparks, 1989 cited in Liebling, 1992); an accusation frequently levelled at ethnographers (Lee 1995). Being young and female and working in a smaller environment may have helped to avoid this. Only one woman suggested I could be a 'cop' or a 'screw'. The question of whether being young and female mattered concerned me throughout. The simple answer to this question is yes. Like Easterday *et al* (1982) and Gelsthorpe (1990), I found being young and female can be both enabling and constraining. It helped to facilitate access. It would have been almost impossible for a male researcher to gain access to women-only spaces. Being young was an advantage in the sense that many of the women prisoners and hostel residents were a similar age to myself. At times it led to the research being described as another student project which I felt to be almost a dismissal of its importance. However, the staff did consider me as a credible researcher and they endorsed the choice of methods, particularly the willingness to spend long periods of time in the setting watching what went on and participating in the action. In particular, one hostel worker commented

> You could ask me what I've been doing in the last half hour and I'd say looking at a map and doing some sums, but it means nothing unless you know that a resident has been offered a job and needs to know how to get there and if they would be better off than if they were claiming benefits
>
> (Fieldnotes: North Street Hostel)

Whilst staff endorsed the choice of methods, throughout the fieldwork I experienced contradictions between accounts, including critical feminist accounts, of how research should be done and my own experiences of it. I oscillated between feeling that these accounts were flawed in some way and feelings of incompetence. In particular, I was concerned about the ethical dilemmas and emotional effects of research with women in criminal justice institutions.

At the design stages, I had chosen methods which I felt to be compatible with the central agenda of feminist social science and scholarship. Like Stacey (1988, p.21), 'I was eager for a 'hands on', face-to-face research experience, which I also believed was more compatible with feminist principles'. However, like Stacey, I became increasingly concerned with this compatibility. I felt my presence among women, described by staff as 'in crisis', to be intrusive and exploitative. This feeling has been described by other researchers. As Glesne and Peshkin (1992, p.112) note,

> Questions of exploitation ... tend to arise as you become immersed in the research and begin to rejoice in the richness of what you are learning. You are thankful but, instead of simply appreciating the gift, you may feel guilty for how much you are receiving and how much you are giving in return.

Asking myself the question of who benefits, I felt that ultimately I was the one to benefit from the research, often resulting in feelings of guilt. Perhaps this feeling was heightened because I was very aware of how the research relationship was inevitably an unequal one. However, what has to be acknowledged is that the research participants did have choices: to participate, to answer questions. Ethnographers have to request and

120

negotiate access (Hammersley, 1992). However, as I have already noted, when conducting ethnographic research in a criminal justice institution these issues are extremely problematic.

At the interview stage of the research, issues of informed consent were less problematic. Drawing upon critical methodological comments made by feminists, I tried to create a relationship based on informality, friendship and collaboration. The women I spoke to talked freely about their lives and experiences, revealing personal information even though I had given them the option not to answer any questions they felt uncomfortable with. It was usually easy to establish rapport on the basis of having something in common, no matter how small, such as having lived in the same area, having a university degree or knowing about the criminal justice system. Feminists suggest that the interviews should involve an exchange of information. Even in the early stages of the research I sensed that the women would want more than to answer my questions. The women were continually questioned about their lives by criminal justice, legal and social welfare professionals. Consequently, their expectations from the research were high. They wanted someone to talk to who would listen and answer their questions. One comment from a woman in a remand centre in particular brought this to light: 'I'd be interested to hear your views unless you've only come here to collect information'. This could be viewed as a plea for emotional involvement and/or request for information from a credible source. Crucially, it made me reflect upon my level of personal involvement in the project, but also the personal investment of taking part in the research.

The fieldwork proved to be a distressing experience for me. I heard stories of violence, poverty, substance abuse and childhood experiences, and learnt something of the difficulties of waiting for trial. I witnessed first hand the impact of drug and alcohol abuse, women with injuries caused by violence; and the depression, anger and anxiety which flow from waiting for trial. A visit to a remand centre was particularly distressing when a woman came up to me and held in front of me her self-mutilated wrists. The goal of objectivity was not one I aspired to and certainly not one I could maintain. As Kleinmann and Copp (1993) argue, qualitative researchers receive mixed messages. At the same time as they are told to work to establish rapport, they are told also to avoid unnecessary emotion and over-identification.

The women showed a diversity of emotions when telling their stories. Some became upset and began to cry, others talked in an angry way and others appeared not to show any emotions at all. The research may have been empowering, an opportunity for women to articulate their experience in the hope that it would lead to change, or it may have been cathartic, providing an outlet for individuals to off-load. More simply, they may have provided women with an opportunity to talk to another interested individual. These potentially positive aspects had to be reconciled with a very real fear that in some way I had caused harm, dredging up painful memories for women already experiencing a difficult period in their lives. Whilst I could listen as they told their stories, I was conscious of my limitations. I was not a therapist, trained counsellor, or medical practitioner. I was particularly wary about offering reassurances about future sentencing outcomes. One young woman with a small child whom she cared for alone confided in me that she would not be able to cope with a prison sentence and asked for my opinion on what would happen to her. I hoped that given her personal circumstances and lack of previous convictions that she would not get a custodial sentence but I could not be certain of this. I carried on listening to her fears and answered only factual questions such as 'what is a probation order?'. At a professional level I knew this was the 'right' thing to do, but on a personal level I felt the need to offer assurances as one might do for a friend.

This reflexive account has explored a number of recurring themes: the importance of gender, ethical considerations and the emotional impact of conducting ethnographic research. Some of these issues have been well documented by researchers, for example, the role of gender. Others, such as the role of emotions, have been marginalised.

Constructing an ethnographic account

The data collected through ethnographic fieldwork is voluminous and recalcitrant. After several months in the field, I had amassed fieldnotes, interview transcripts, analytic memos and a variety of documents. Concentrated data analysis began after leaving the field but as Hammersley and Atkinson (1995) argue, the data analysis process is not a distinct stage in itself but begins with entry to the field and continues throughout the research. Writing is central to the data analysis process.

> Writing makes us think about data in new and different ways. Thinking about how to represent our data also forces us to think about the meanings and understandings, voices and experiences present in the data ... Analytic ideas are developed and tried out in the process of writing and representing
> (Coffey and Atkinson, 1996, p.109).

The key issue here is representation. Earlier in this chapter, recent critiques of the ability of ethnographic texts to 'tell it like it is' were discussed. Authors need to be conscious that they are not telling the stories the actors themselves would have told or simply presenting their findings, they are creating accounts of social life. The ethnographer is both storyteller and scientist (Fetterman, 1989), offering 'thick description' (Geertz, 1973), with rich and detailed descriptive accounts presented around an analytic framework. The fieldnotes and other sources of data gathered are reconstructed as a narrative which is accessible to another audience.

All ethnographic texts aim to persuade the reader that their account is authentic, and thus they are constructed with a particular audience in mind. For example, the research on which this chapter is based has been written up as a PhD thesis, journal articles for professional and academic audiences, chapters in academic books, and reports to probation services. The same material can be presented in different ways in order to reach diverse audiences (Richardson, 1990). I have yet to experiment with theatrical scripts (Ellis and Bochner, 1992; Mienczakowski, 1996) or poetry (Richardson, 1992)! If feminist research is concerned with making women's lives visible and listening to women's voices, then the need to disseminate research findings is heightened, as is the potential need to involve women fully in the production of the ethnographic account.

The collaborative model proposed by Duelli Klein (1983) and Mies (1983), which involves encouraging women to participate in the process of analysis and writing, is problematic (Stacey, 1988). For this research project is was not appropriate. Women prisoners and hostel residents could not be easily reached after the research had ended, although feedback was sought from the women who worked with them. However, the use of language that women use to describe their own lives and the inclusion of quotations were strategies used to establish the text as a sociology for, rather than about women. Such strategies are not totally unproblematic. Only offering short 'snippets' may fragment, even distort, individual experiences (Atkinson, 1992). Whilst conscious of this, I was faced with an ethical dilemma. The inclusion of detailed discussion about the lives of individual women may lead to them being identified. There are few remand centres and bail hostels for women and some of the women interviewed were charged with offences which had resulted in media attention. My desire to protect the confidentiality of the women I had met thus influenced the way my ethnographic account was constructed. This illustrates the ways in which the dilemmas faced by feminist ethnographers impact on the research process from the initial stages through to the production of an ethnographic account and perhaps beyond.

Concluding comments

Reinharz (1992) suggests that feminist ethnographers typically make double contributions when they conduct their research. They contribute to our understanding of feminist ethnography as a method of social research, and they contribute to our understanding of the subject matter they choose to study. Every feminist ethnographic project generates its own new set of concerns, in addition to touching on familiar ones. Within this chapter, I have focused on the dilemmas of feminist ethnography raised by researchers such as Reinharz (1992) and Stacey (1988) as they relate to my own research. I have also suggested that there are further dilemmas which relate to feminist fieldwork in criminal justice institutions. My research findings and contribution to the 'patchwork' (Heidensohn, 1994) of feminist criminological knowledge are explored elsewhere (Wincup 1996; 1997; 1998a; 1998b).

Despite the controversies and dilemmas within feminist ethnography, ethnographic research has enormous potential to make visible women's lives in general, and the lives of women who appear before the courts in particular. In the research reported in this chapter, the blend of different research methodologies worked well. Through participant observation, I was able to build up rapport with research participants and to get a sense of the key issues relevant to women's experiences of waiting for trial and the everyday world of bail hostels and remand centres. Through interviews, I was able to ask questions on emergent themes from the observational period of the research. Reflecting on the data I have leads me to agree with Olesen's (1995, p.169) conclusion that 'the complexities and problems of women's lives, whatever the context, are sufficiently great that multiple approaches via qualitative research are required'.

Inevitably, numerous questions are raised throughout the research process which require reflection upon. Such reflections can be used in ways which enhance rather than downgrade feminist ethnography. The long tradition of ethnography within criminological research implies the appropriateness of this methodological approach to researching issues of crime and criminal justice. As criminology moves towards becoming a gendered discipline, there is scope to follow in this tradition incorporating the insights of feminist methodological debates and exploring issues of gender in relation to crime and criminal justice.

References

Adler, P. and Adler, P. (1995) 'The Demography of Ethnography', *Journal of Contemporary Ethnography*, 24, pp. 3-29.

Anthias, F. and Yuval-Davis, A. (1983) 'Contextualizing Feminism: Gender, Ethnic and Class Divisions', *Feminist Review*, 5, pp. 62-73.

Atkinson, P. (1990) *The Ethnographic Imagination: Textual Constructions of Reality*, Routledge, London.

Atkinson, P. (1992) *Understanding Ethnographic Texts*, Sage, Newbury Park, Ca.

Becker, H. (1963) *Outsiders*, The Free Press, New York.

Carlen, P. (1985) (ed) *Criminal Women: Autobiographical Accounts*, Polity Press, Cambridge.

Carlen, P. (1994) 'Why Study Women's Imprisonment or Anyone Else's?, *British Journal of Criminology*, 31, pp. 131-40

Carter, K. (1995) *The Occupational Socialisation of Prison Officers, An Ethnography*, Unpublished PhD Thesis, University of Wales, Cardiff.

Clifford, J. and Marcus, G. (1986) (eds) *Writing Culture: The Poetics and Politics of Ethnography*, University of California Press, Berkeley, Ca.

Clough, P. (1992) *The Ends of Ethnography*, Sage, Newbury Park, Ca.

Coffey, A. and Atkinson, P. (1996) *Making Sense of Qualitative Data*, Sage, London.

Denzin, N. (1997) *Interpretive Ethnography: Ethnographic Practices for the 21st Century*, Sage, Thousand Oaks, Ca.

Duelli-Klein, R. (1983) 'How To Do What We Do: Thoughts About Feminist Methodology', in Bowles, G. and Duelli-Klein, R. (eds), *Theories of Women's Studies*, Routledge, London.

Easterday, L., Paperdemas, D., Schorr, L. and Valentine, C. (1982) 'The Making of a Female Researcher: Some Role Problems in Fieldwork', in Burgess, R. (ed), *Field Research, A Sourcebook and Field Manual*, Allen and Unwin, London.

Eaton, M. (1986) *Justice for Women, Family, Court and Social Control*, Open University Press, Buckingham.

Ellis, C. and Bochner, A. (1992) 'Telling and Performing Personal Stories, The Constraints of Choice in Abortion', in Ellis, C. and Flaherty, G. (eds) *Investigating Subjectivity: Research on Lived Experience*, Sage, Newbury Park, Ca.

Fetterman, M. (1989) *Ethnography: Step by Step*, Sage, Newbury Park Ca.

Finch, J. (1984) 'It's Great to Have Someone to Talk to', in Bell, C. and Roberts, H. (eds) *Social Researching: Politics, Problems, Practice*, Routledge, London.

Geer, B. (1964) 'First Days in the Field', in Hammond, P. (ed) *Sociologists at Work: Essays on the Craft of Social Research*, Basic Books, New York.

Geertz, C. (1973) 'Thick Description', in Geertz, C. (ed), *The Interpretation of Cultures*, Basic Books, New York.

Gelsthorpe, L. (1990) 'Feminist Methodologies in Criminology: A New Approach or Old Wine in New Bottles?', in Gelsthorpe, L. and Morris, A. (eds), *Feminist Perspectives in Criminology*, Open University Press, Buckingham.

Gelsthorpe, L. and Morris, A. (1990) *Feminist Perspectives in Criminology*, Open University Press, Buckingham.

Gold, R. (1958) 'Roles in Sociological Observation', *Social Forces*, 36, pp. 217-223.

Glesne, C. and Peshkin, A. (1992) *Becoming Qualitative Researchers*, White Plains, Longman, New York.

Graham, H. (1984) 'Surveying Through Stories', in Bell, C. and Roberts, H. (eds) *Social Researching: Politics, Problems, Practice*, Routledge, London.

Hammersley, M. (1992) *What's Wrong with Ethnography*, Routledge, London.

Hammersley, M. and Atkinson, P. (1995) *Ethnography: Principles in Practice*, Routledge, London.

Heidensohn, F. (1994) *Feminist Criminologies: Directions for the Future*, Unpublished, Paper Presented to the Institute of Criminology, Cambridge.

Hill Collins, P. (1990) *Black Feminist Thought: Knowledge, Consciousness and the Politics of Empowerment*, Unwin Hyman, London.

Hobbs, D. (1988) *Doing the Business: Entrepreneurship, The Working Class and Detectives in the East End of London*, Oxford University Press, Oxford.

Kelly, L. (1990) 'Journeying in Reverse: Possibilities and Problems in Feminist Research on Sexual Violence', in Gelsthorpe, L. and Morris, A. (eds), *Feminist Perspectives in Criminology*, Open University Press, Buckingham.

Kelly, L., Regan, L. and Burton, S. (1992) 'Defending the Indefensible? Quantitative Methods and Feminist Research', in Hinds, H., Phoenix, A. and Stacey, J. (eds), *Working Out: New Directions in Women's Studies*, Falmer Press, London.

Kleinmann, S. and Copp, M. (1993) *Emotions and Fieldwork*, Sage, Newbury Park, Ca.

Lee, R. (1995) *Dangerous Fieldwork*, Thousand Oaks, Sage, Ca.

Liebling, A. (1992) *Suicides in Prison*, Routledge, London.

Lofland, L. (1987) 'Reflections on a Thrice-named Journal', *Journal of Contemporary Ethnography*, 16, pp. 25-40.

Manning, P. (1987) 'The Ethnographic Conceit', *Journal of Contemporary Ethnography*, 16, pp. 49-68.

Marcus, G. and Fischer, M. (1986) *Anthropology as Cultural Critique: An Experimental Moment in the Human Sciences*, University of Chicago Press, Chicago.

Marshall, C. and Rossman, G. (1989) *Designing Qualitative Research*, Sage, Newbury Park, Ca.

May, T. (1991) *Probation: Politics, Policy and Practice*, Open University Press, Buckingham.

Maynard, M. and Purvis, J. (1994) *Researching Women's Lives from a Feminist Perspective*, Taylor and Francis, London.

Mienczakowski, J. (1996) *An Ethnographic Act: The Construction of Consensual Theatre and the Representation of Research Results*, Unpublished, Paper Presented to the 4th International Conference on Social Science Research Methodology, University of Essex.

Mies, M. (1983) 'Towards a Methodology for Feminist Research', in Bowles, G. and Duelli-Klein, R. (eds), *Theories of Women's Studies*, Routledge, London.

Oakley, A. (1981) 'Interviewing Women: A Contradiction in Terms', in Roberts, H. (ed) *Doing Feminist Research*, Routledge, London.

Olesen, V. (1994) 'Feminisms and Models of Qualitative Research', in Denzin, N, and Lincoln, Y. (eds.) *The Handbook of Qualitative Research*, Sage, Newbury Park, Ca.

Padel, U. and Stevenson, J. (1988) *Insiders: Women's Experiences of Imprisonment*, Virago, London.

Pearson, G. (1993) 'Talking a Good Fight: Authenticity and Distance in the Ethnographer's Craft', in Hobbs, D. and May, T (eds.), *Interpreting the Field: Accounts of Ethnography*, Oxford University Press, Oxford.

Peckham, A. (1985) *A Woman in Custody*, Fontana, London.

Pugh, A. (1990) 'My Statistics and Feminism - A True Story', in Stanley, L. (ed), *Feminist Praxis: Research Theory and Epistemology in Feminist Sociology*, Routledge, London.

Reinharz, S. (1992) *Feminist Methods in Social Research*, Oxford University Press, New York.

Rice, M. (1990) 'Challenging Orthodoxies in Feminist Theory: A Black Feminist Critique', in Gelsthorpe, L. and Morris, A. (eds), *Feminist Perspectives in Criminology*, Open University Press, Buckingham.

Richardson, L. (1990) *Writing Strategies: Reaching Diverse Audiences*, Sage, Newbury Park, Ca.

Richardson, L. (1992) 'The Consequences of Poetic Representation: Writing the Other, Writing the Self', in Ellis, C. and Flaherty, G. (eds), *Investigating Subjectivity: Research on Lived Experience*, Sage, Newbury Park, Ca.

Roberts, H. (1981) (ed) *Doing Feminist Research*, Routledge, London.

Rock, P. (1993) *The Social World of an English Crown Court*, Clarendon Press, Oxford.

Roseneil, S. (1993) 'Greenham Revisited: Researching Myself and My Sisters', in Hobbs, D. and May, T. (eds) *Interpreting the Field: Accounts of Ethnography*, Oxford University Press, Oxford.

Schwartz, M. and Schwartz, C. (1955) 'Problems in Participant Observation', *American Journal of Sociology*, 36, pp. 217-33.

Skeggs, B. (1994) 'Situating the Production of Feminist Ethnography', in Maynard, M. and Purvis, J. (eds), *Researching Women's Lives from a Feminist Perspective*, Taylor and Francis, London.

Smart, C. (1990) 'Feminist Approaches to Criminology or Postmodern Woman Meets Atavistic Man', in Gelsthorpe, L. and Morris, A. (eds), *Feminist Perspectives in Criminology*, Open University Press, Buckingham.

Spelman, E. (1990) *Inessential Women: Problems of Exclusion in Feminist Thought*, The Women's Press, London.

Stacey, J. (1988) 'Can There be a Feminist Ethnography?', *Women's Studies International Quarterly*, 11, pp. 21-27.

Stanley, L. and Wise, S. (1993) *Breaking Out Again: Feminist Consciousness and Feminist Research*, Routledge, London.

Thrasher, F. (1927) The Gang: A Study of 1,313 Gangs in Chicago, University of Chicago Press, Chicago.

Van Maanen, J. (1991) 'Playing Back the Tape: Early Days in the Field', in Shaffir, W. and Stebbins, R. (eds), *Experiencing Fieldwork*, Sage, Newbury Park, Ca.

Wincup, E. (1996) 'Mixed Hostels, Staff and Resident Perspectives', *Probation Journal*, 43, pp. 147-51.

Wincup, E. (1997) *Waiting for Trial, Living and Working in a Bail Hostel*, Unpublished PhD Thesis, University of Wales, Cardiff.

Wincup, E. (1998a) 'Managing Uncertainty, Women's Experiences of Waiting for Trial', *Social Science Teacher*, 27, pp. 8-12.

Wincup, E. (1998b) 'Power, Control and the Gendered Body, Coping Strategies and Women's Lives', in Richardson, J. and Shaw, A. (eds), *The Body in Qualitative Research*, Ashgate, Aldershot.

Wolf, M. (1992) *A Thrice-told Tale: Feminism, Postmodernism and Ethnographic Responsibility*, Stanford University Press, Stanford, Ca.

8   Oral history and the cultures of the police

Tom Cockcroft

Introduction

Since the 1960s the study of cop culture has provided social scientists with an array of fascinating ethnographies which have added to our understanding of police work. Authors such as Skolnick (1966), Manning (1977), and Holdaway (1983) have helped define and develop the framework which became the standard when researching the culture of the police. However, an over reliance on such approaches has led to numerous pieces of research which succeed in proving that some police officers sometimes display negative traits such as racism, sexism, and dishonesty. Such negative attributes are then taken as the norm amongst officers and ascribed as being the effect of some overwhelming culture. This, in itself, does not constitute an altogether helpful approach to the issue of cop culture as it lays itself wide open to criticisms of simplicity.

Chan (1996) criticises this over-simplistic approach to cop culture and criticised existing approaches on a number of grounds. Primarily, Chan argues that we should look to the existence of multiple police cultures, rather than an homogenous culture shared by all officers, regardless of rank. Her second criticism addresses the way in which police officers are portrayed as being the passive recipients of the cultural code and being unable to resist its all encompassing effect. Thirdly, Chan claims that existing literature on cop culture failed to appreciate the social, political, legal and organisational context of policing. Chan's final criticism relates to the idea that current theorising offers an all-powerful, homogenous and deterministic conception of police culture and therefore does not allow discussion of the possibility of cultural change.

Background to the research

It is with such ideas in mind that the research discussed in this chapter was undertaken. Whilst acknowledging a great debt to the previous literature in the area, it was recognised that there was a need to adopt the type of flexibility proposed by Chan. The starting point was one that endeavoured to show that whilst certain aspects of police culture have remained constant over a historical period, it is perhaps now problematic to think in terms of a single culture. Despite the existence of many cultural reference points within the policing profession, it is important to acknowledge that these are neither fixed nor deterministic. Research has pointed to the fact that different cultural dynamics emerge within different parts of the police hierarchy; for example, the work of Reuss-Ianni and Ianni (1983) who distinguished between the respective cultural dynamics of 'street cop culture' and 'management cop culture'. My research supports the thinking that the cultural dynamics of the police can be broken down further, even to the extent where different reliefs (shifts) within the same station embrace different cultural reference points and therefore could be said to adhere to different cultures. Such a view is made possible only if one accepts the notion that police culture is fluid and malleable rather than monolithic and deterministic. Similarly, we need to accept the possibility that individual officers are granted some degree of free will in their actions rather than embracing, without question, apparently determined (and therefore unavoidable) attitudes and behaviours.

In order to explore the idea of the fluidity of police culture, especially when compared over time and between places, semi-structured interviews were conducted with 26 ex-police officers (23 male and 3 female) who had joined the ranks of the Metropolitan Police Force between the years of 1930 and 1960. The research was limited to officers who served between those years as it was thought it would be unfeasible to gain access to any officers who had joined prior to that date. The research was limited to the Metropolitan Police Force Area because it was envisaged that such a boundary encompasses many different environments and thus, many different opportunities for diverse policing practices and cultural dynamics.

The research was limited to the option of oral history as there was, I believe, no feasible alternative methodological technique which would draw the information which was required. Gaining information on policing from as far back as the 1930s would otherwise necessitate the use of existing historical texts which would fail to take into account officers' own views concerning policing in that period. Prior to the initiation of this study, it was decided to keep the use of historical texts, which would largely offer 'orthodox' or conventional accounts, to a minimum and to rely on oral histories and journal entries. Bloch (1954) investigated the dichotomy between unearthed traces (i.e. historical 'facts') and oral histories, a distinction first made by anthropologists and later investigated by social historians. Trace histories have traditionally been held in higher estimation due to the prevailing influence of the paradigm of scientific positivism. Tonkin (1992) expanded upon this point when she wrote, 'in an academic culture of objectivity, this is their moral charm. They are purely impersonal' (p.84). Thus, the evolution of oral history is characterised by an on-going struggle against the assumption that 'facts' gained from trace history may be seen as objective and oral histories as subjective. Increasingly oral histories, like qualitative research in general, are being viewed as a valid account of social reality.

Firstly, it was necessary to formulate the areas of police occupational culture that I wished to address during the semi-structured interviews. Unsurprisingly, the research addressed 'traditional' correlates of police culture such as camaraderie, the 'cult of masculinity' (Fielding, 1994 and Gray, 1983), attitudes to women and minority groups, corruption, and so forth. However, attention was also given to the differentiation of officers' views and recollections on topics such as the dynamics of police/public relationships and how it differed between both police stations and areas; officers' relationships with 'villains', with magistrates, and the relationship between uniform and CID officers amongst others. By doing so I hoped to be able to construct a picture of police culture over a 30 year period informed, not just by common observation over a relatively short time, but through in-depth discussions with officers who were willing, not just to explain their actions but, also to attach *meanings* to such actions. Additionally their status as ex-police officers may have resulted in a willingness to be more open and revealing in the accounts provided.

One example which serves to illustrate this point is that of 'corruption'. I would argue that corruption within the police force often appears to be analysed in a rather two-dimensional way. Police officers have been seen as engaging in what may be termed 'bad practice' in order to 'get results'. The findings from my research indicate a different picture. For example, ex-officers who were interviewed indicated how there has, historically, within certain parts of the Metropolitan Police Force been a tendency for some officers to commit perjury in court. To many, this serves, merely, as evidence that police officers may be portrayed as dishonest and corrupt. Such an analysis fails to account for the cultural rule of the police that states that one only 'gilds the lily' when one 'knows' that the defendant is guilty. This practice was linked directly to the widespread belief amongst officers that the criminal justice system is loaded against the police and that it favours the criminal. As such the police are not necessarily motivated in their actions by any deep-rooted biases against certain groups, but by disillusionment with a system that inhibits them in the execution of their agenda, namely the protection of individuals and property. One PC articulated the views of many

132

of the interviewees when he said:

> But the thing I always remember...that when you had a job of arresting somebody which sometimes was a bit dodgy in as much that the person who had committed the crime...you knew full well...you had to stretch the evidence a bit. To get a conviction you could rely a hundred per cent on whatever you said would be backed up by your fellow officer. It didn't matter who it was. You sort of had a...you could rely on one another but the thing was you never, ever got an innocent man down. If you knew that person was guilty you did anything you could do to make sure that he was convicted...but you never, ever stretched it a bit to get an innocent man in the dock

Similarly, many analyses neglect to address the personal dimensions of policework and the fact that some officers might, in retrospect, regret the outcome of the use of the often arbitrary aspects of policing such as the use (and misuse) of Section 66 of the Metropolitan Police Act (stop and search powers or what are commonly termed 'sus' laws). As one retired CID officer stated:

> I think anyone who's a decent person and has worked in the CID...especially at that time...can't look back without regretting a lot of the stuff they've done...a lot of it was wrong but we were young and we thought what we were doing was right

Bearing the complexity of police culture in mind, it was felt appropriate to use oral histories to gain an understanding of officers' different views and experiences. However the use of oral histories is not totally unproblematic, as other researchers have noted (Seldon and Pappworth, 1983). In the remainder of this chapter I will chart the main issues which came to light during the research, with a particular focus upon the definitive observations of Seldon and Papperworth. In short, I will focus upon my own experiences of the strengths and weaknesses of this methodological approach.

Dilemmas of oral history techniques

Disadvantages of the oral history technique fall, generally, into two main categories; those attributable to the interviewee and those attributable to the interviewer. Interviewee-based disadvantages include factors, according to

Seldon and Pappworth, such as the 'unreliability of memory', 'excessive discretion', 'lack of perspective', 'self-consciousness', and the 'influence of hindsight'. Collectively these reflect factors which inhibit the interviewee from accurately recollecting what happened in the past.

The age of some of the interviewees who participated in this research might have had an adverse effect upon their ability to recall events. However, such concerns appeared to be largely unfounded. None of the respondents appeared to experience difficulty in recalling events from, in some cases, over fifty years ago. However it must be noted that it is extremely difficult to gauge the extent to which gaps in memory are 'filled' through information which has come to light in the years following the original occurrence and this is a factor which must be borne in mind by all researchers engaged in oral history research (Andrews, 1993; Collins et al., 1993). The view of memory as reconstruction rather than reproduction is also discussed in chapter one of this volume.

The problem of 'excessive discretion' did, unsurprisingly, occur on a number of occasions mainly when the interview focused upon the issue of corruption. More surprisingly, though, was the fact that several of the officers were extremely frank and were prepared to divulge information regarding the existence of corrupt or, to be more accurate, 'bad' police practice. Such information, when divulged, was extremely important as it chronicled not only the actuality of police indiscretions but also the meanings which the individual officers attached to such behaviours.

It is difficult to assess to what extent the ex-officers exhibited a 'lack of perspective' and underplayed the role of wider factors but generally, those officers who were interviewed appeared to have a wide grasp of policing and its role in society. In many ways, it could be argued that police officers are ideally placed to view both their occupation and the milieu within which it operates in an analytical manner. As an example, one ex-PC, whilst talking on the theme of the police relationship with the public, said:

> Looking back at Grunwick...a union dispute...it was sort of pre-Arthur Scargill with his flying pickets and that kind of thing...and there was a polarising of the police and the public...I think it's here to this day...the public are out there...the police are here...and it's like a necessary evil that we have to have

Such a comment provides evidence to support the view that police officers are able to view their working lives with a degree of perspective that betrays a shrewd knowledge of the world they inhabit. The above statement displays an awareness of the way in which public order policing has far-reaching effects on the state of police/public relations. Similarly, it acknowledges an understanding of the way in which the perception of the police has shifted from one of 'civilians in uniform' to one of 'necessary evil'. It may be the case that former officers are able to distance themselves from their former profession and give a balanced view which is less hindered by notions of 'occupational loyalty' than would otherwise be the case.

Another disadvantage, identified by Seldon and Pappworth, which is more difficult to both control for and identify is that of the influence of hindsight. Oral history is, by its very nature, attempting to unearth how people felt during the period they are talking about and not how they may have interpreted such feelings in the light of more recent evidence and experiences. It is impossible to control for the effects of hindsight and it is hoped that the individuals in question will place more faith in their own feelings about an occurrence as it happened rather than someone else's subsequent interpretation.

Oral history in practice

Seldon and Pappworth also addressed a number of disadvantages of the oral history technique which are interviewer or methodology-based. Those which may have affected this research will be considered, namely, 'unrepresentative sampling', 'biased questioning', 'deference and bias towards interviewees', and 'interviews as a replacement for reading documents'. These are issues for qualitative research in general and are not limited to the oral history method.

Oral historians usually rely on samples which are somewhat opportunistic. Thus, one criticism of this method is that the sample may be perceived as unrepresentative. Broadly speaking, my sample predominantly included officers who had joined the Metropolitan Police Force in the 1930s and 1940s. With hindsight, this research may have benefited from interviewing approximately equal numbers of officers who served during different decades between the 1930s and 1960s. This would allow the researcher to capture possible variations in the experience of serving officers during this important period in the development of the modern police force (Emsley, 1991). Another possible criticism of this research relates to the representation of female ex-officers within the sample. Of the twenty-six officers who consented to be interviewed, only three were female. Whilst not unrepresentative of the gender makeup of the Metropolitan Police Force during this historical period, an increased representation of female ex-officers may have provided vital information about this male dominated profession. This is just one example of the compromises researchers make when conducting qualitative research.

Further compromises relate to the constraints of both time and resources. For instance, it became necessary on some occasions to adopt a different approach from the typical one to one interview format. Twice I had to interview two ex-officers at the same time to avoid the expense of two lengthy trips. Such interviews proved problematic for a number of reasons. Generally one of the interviewees would adopt a dominant role and tend to monopolise the interview making it harder for the interviewer to gain the views of the other, more passive, interviewee. Additionally it was often difficult to control the dynamics of the interview and direct the flow of conversation, particularly when ex-officers began reminiscing amongst themselves; although of course this was very valuable data.

Seldon and Pappworth examined the issue of biased questioning and how it may affect the validity of a particular study. This, of course, applies to all forms of interview and questionnaires and has to be addressed by any researcher utilising such methodological tools (O'Connell Davidson and Layder, 1994). Taking this point to its extreme, one might argue that merely by asking a question one is introducing an element of bias into a situation, by drawing another individual's conscious thought to a specific area, solely determined by the interviewer. One common strategy to address this problem, frequently adopted in the case of oral histories, is to undertake an unstructured interview (May, 1997).

Deference and bias towards interviewees is seen as a common problem which occurs during oral history interviews, which is exacerbated when interviewing individuals who are famous or of high status. During the research this was not seen as a major factor although, it has to be said, that there was a tendency on the side of the interviewer, during the earlier interviews, to exhibit slightly more deference to the subjects than in later interviews. It is, perhaps, inevitable that the interviewer's confidence increases throughout the course of twenty-five interviews as does their ability to draw the desired information out of the respondent. With regards to this research, certain aspects of policing between the 1930s and the 1960s have not been documented, to my knowledge, in any existing texts and certain areas of policing only came to my knowledge throughout the course of the interviews. This resulted in much more informed interviewing taking place in the later interviews by virtue of the fact that I had acquired a greater amount of knowledge.

Seldon and Pappworth's final concern relates to an over-reliance by oral historians on the spoken word at the expense of written documentary evidence. This did not apply to this research for two main reasons. Firstly, although, it may be argued that background materials may provide a basic understanding of the structure and organisation of policing at the time, there is very little existing academic literature relating to the occupational culture of the Metropolitan Police between the 1930s and the 1960s. More importantly, this research was largely concerned not only with the behaviour of officers (which existing sources may attempt to chart) but also with the meanings which individual officers attribute to those behaviours. The use of qualitative oral histories appears the most appropriate approach when one adopts this theoretical stance.

Advantages of oral history

Seldon and Pappworth list a number of advantages specific to the oral history methodology. Those which were relevant to the present study will now be addressed. These advantages can be seen as adhering to the categories of 'gaps in documentation', 'underlying assumptions and motives', 'atmosphere and colour', and 'discovery of entirely new information'. Generally, these advantages refer to the ways in which oral history can provide researchers with another dimension to our understanding of, in this case, the culture of the police. In other words, a greater depth of understanding is gained by the assimilation of views or opinions of certain past behaviours or occurrences in relation to more recent changes in policing.

Primarily, it may be said that this research benefited from the oral history technique in that it succeeded in filling significant gaps in existing knowledge. Very few existing documents shed any light on police occupational culture as far back as the 1930s and the 1940s. Oral history was the only research tool that could succeed in generating such information. Similarly, oral history allows us to question the validity of existing accounts of policing. Most of the literature concerning the police between the 1930s and the 1950s represents an orthodox or establishment view of policing and oral history allows us to contrast this view of policework with oral testimonies of the officers themselves. There is, however, a potential danger. Eagerness to produce an authentic social history may lead to the outright rejection of any material which has come from an orthodox source. This is as damaging as assuming that all oral testimonies are non-problematic.

Much of the literature of policing is based upon ethnographic accounts which involve the researcher's interpretation of particular current events and actions (Hobbs, 1988; Norris, 1993). Consequently such an approach is unable to provide us with an historical perspective. Oral histories allow us to see how ex-officers themselves view their own actions and how they interpret them within their own understanding of policework. Whilst it is impossible to

137

lose the researcher's own frame of reference, the oral history method does give a direct voice to those who have experienced policing in a different era. Of course, this is not to say that academic researchers have little to contribute to our understanding of policework nor that the views of individual officers should be taken as being the definitive analysis of policework. What is proposed is that we should question the validity of assuming that all officers are passive actors within the social context of policing and that their understanding is ultimately flawed by virtue of their being directly involved in the processes being studied.

Seldon and Pappworth also noted that oral history is useful in that it provides accounts of various happenings with a sense of 'atmosphere and colour'. This proved to be very much the case during my research. Oral histories, once transcribed, tend to give a much more 'realistic' and readable account of a certain happening when compared to a 'dry' piece of documentary evidence. Such histories, by providing us with a personal dimension, allow a richer appreciation, especially when investigating the relationship between the public and the police. One example of the 'colour' which oral history can give to a subject arose when a retired PC began talking about the isolation and alienation felt by many officers. He said:

> Colin McInnes...who wrote 'Mr Love and Mr Justice'...his attitude towards coppers that both coppers and criminals have a sadness about their lives is true...it's true that when you leave the police you rejoin the human race

A further advantage of oral history is the possibility of discovering entirely new information. Frequently, during interviews, incidents would be recounted which were of particular interest to those researching the cultures of the police and many of which would not have been reported to anyone other than work colleagues or, possibly, intimate individuals in their personal lives. Such occasions gave me the impression that I was being entrusted with information which had previously never been documented and gave an important insight into the typically 'closed' world of policing.

It appears impossible to successfully resolve the inherent conflicts surrounding the use of oral history techniques. Ultimately, the argument can be simplified to one of objectivity versus subjectivity. Methodological criticisms generally come from those who subscribe to a paradigm which stresses the importance of objectivity. Such critics might ask, 'How do we know that the interviewee is telling the truth?' or 'Is the interviewer competent enough?' Those who propose the use of oral history techniques, are not concerned with creating objective accounts, but rather seek to gather data which reflects the richness of human recollections on a particular subject.

In conclusion, it must be stated that oral history techniques provide researchers with a valid alternative to the conventional historical tools which utilise existing documents, often producing orthodox accounts. Additionally, the use of oral history techniques gives a voice to those members of society, in this case ex-police officers, who are often excluded from contributing their knowledge, beliefs and experience towards historical academic endeavours. The accounts provided can create a 'history from below'. In some cases, this research method may be viewed, unfairly, as a last resort to be utilised under duress when no other documentary data presents itself to be analysed. However, if used appropriately and reflexively, oral history techniques are adept at providing us with rich, detailed and meaningful accounts of police cultures in years past.

References

Andrews, M. (1993) *Lifetimes of Commitment: Ageing, Politics, Psychology,* Cambridge University Press, Cambridge.

Bloch, M. (1954) *The Historian's Craft* (tr. Putnam, P.), Manchester University Press, Manchester.

Chan, J. (1996) 'Changing Police Culture'. *British Journal of Criminology,* 36 (1), pp. 109-134.

Collins, A., Gathercole, S., Conway, M. and Morris, P. (1993) *Theories of Memory,* Lawrence Eelbaum Associates,. Hove.

Emsley, C. (1991) *The English Police: A Political and Social History,* Harvester Wheatsheaf, Hemel Hemstead.

Fielding, N. (1994) 'Cop Canteen Culture' in Newburn, T. and Stanko, E. (eds), *Just Boys Doing the Business,* Routledge, London.

Hobbs, D. (1988) *Doing the Business: Entrepreneurship, The Working Class and Detectives in the East End of London,* Oxford University Press, Oxford.

Holdaway, S (1983) *Inside The British Police,* Blackwell, Oxford.

Manning, P. (1977) *Police Work,* MIT Press, Cambridge, Mass.

May, T. (1997) *Social Research,* Open University Press, Buckingham.

Norris, C. (1993) 'Some Ethical Considerations in Fieldwork with the Police' in Hobbs, D. and May, T. (eds), *Interpreting the Field: Accounts of Ethnography,* Oxford University Press, Oxford.

O'Connell Davidson, J. and Layder, D. (1994) *Methods, Sex and Madness,* London: Routledge.

Reuss-Ianni, E., and Ianni, F. (1983) 'Street Cops and Management Cops: The Two Cultures of Policing', in Punch, M. (ed), *Control in the Police Organization*, MIT Press, Cambridge, MA.

Seldon, A. and Pappworth, J. (1983) *By Word of Mouth: Elite Oral History*, Methuen, London.

Skolnick, J. (1966) *Justice Without Trial*, Wiley, New York.

Tonkin, E. (1992) *Narrating Our Past: The Social Construction of Oral History*, Cambridge University Press, Cambridge.

9 Cops for hire: methodological issues in researching private policing

Lesley Noaks

Introduction

This chapter is concerned with the emergence of private policing in residential communities in the United Kingdom. While private security services have been a recurrent feature of the commercial sector in recent years (Johnston, 1992; Jones and Newburn, 1998), the extension of private policing into residential areas is a more contemporary trend which has yet to be fully explored by researchers. A patchwork of neighbourhood security patrols operated by a diverse range of commercial companies is appearing throughout the U.K., effecting a radical departure from the traditionally public status of policing and law enforcement (Loader, 1997; Sheptycki, 1997). In the light of this, Wilkie *et al* (1995) suggest that we are in need of an 'urgent review' of the increasing drive toward privatisation of policing and the extent to which it represents 'a fundamental modification of the character, policy and practice of public policing'.

This chapter reviews the methods used to investigate an emerging but as yet under researched activity. In common with most other chapters in the volume the piece represents an account of 'doing sociological research' (Bell and Newby, 1977) intended to inform the reader via a problematisation of the research task. The research project deployed a combination of qualitative and quantitative methods, including a neighbourhood survey, interviews with police personnel and an ethnographic study of a private security firm. The ethnography has been ongoing for a period of 2 years, facilitating attention to the evolution of the company and any change in its status. The focus of the chapter will be the potential for shifting relationships between researcher and informants in an extended period of fieldwork and related issues of negotiation and re-negotiation.

Background to the research

The research project is premised on an acknowledgement of the increasing significance of private security guards as active providers of community law and order. It is evident from research in this area that in an increasing number of communities in Britain the government sponsored drive toward 'active citizenship' has developed into a buying in of enhanced security and patrol services from commercial groups (Loader, 1997). While a variety of models of public/private policing are emerging (Wakefield, 1997), increasingly the role of the public police is supplemented by some form of private policing. Following on from this, my research has identified some level of unwillingness on the part of the public police to formally acknowledge a contribution from the private sector. However, despite any such reluctance, commercially provided private guards are moving beyond their security role in the commercial world and providing neighbourhood patrols, an activity increasingly affording them a higher profile with the general community.

Despite their increasing profile, few published studies have focused on the occupational culture of private policing, with the exception in the U.K. of Johnston (1992) and Newburn and Jones (1998). In contrast, considerable research attention has been paid to the culture of public policing, with much of the work of a qualitative nature and including attention to ethical considerations (Holdaway, 1983; Norris, 1993). The rationale for this project is that the increasing prominence of private police on the criminal justice stage requires a similar focus on their role and the general impact of this form of privatisation of social control. This chapter is based is ongoing research located in an urban residential area, where private security patrols are selectively provided by a commercial company to households who pay into the scheme. The 'patch' covered by the private security firm is on the outer perimeter of a large urban development and consists of a mixture of public and private housing mostly built since the early 1980s. At the time of writing the security company has a director and five security guards, who provide foot and vehicle patrols between 11pm and 6am and an on-call service for subscribers in the early evening.

The broad objectives of the research are to consider the relationship between private and public policing in a specific physical location and the consequences of that for individual residents' constructions of the crime problem and law enforcement in their community. The project has deployed a multi method approach, incorporating both qualitative and quantitative procedures, intended to diversify the routes by which data were gathered:

Community

Neighbourhood surveys were undertaken with both subscribers and non subscribers to the private security scheme. A semi-structured interview schedule, combining closed and open questions, was used in the collection of data. A small team of three interviewers undertook all of the interviews and were encouraged to record responses to the open questions in the respondents own words. The focus of the questionnaire was residents' attitudes to community, including the role of public and private policing and perceptions of the local crime problem, including direct and indirect experiences of victimisation and related fear of crime.

Policing

Interviews have been undertaken with senior police personnel to gauge the strategic policy responses to the emergence of private police in the force area. In conjunction with formal approaches to the police, informal links with police personnel have also been utilised to extend understanding of police responses beyond the officially sanctioned accounts. The focus of such enquiries has been the level of inter-relationship between private and public policing and the potential for enhanced collaboration and partnership. At this stage in the research, the findings reveal some unwillingness on the part of the public police to acknowledge any role for private groups and a situation of stand-off in relation to active co-operation.

Private policing

A major strand of the research has been a qualitative study of the occupational culture of private policing achieved by means of participant observation, in the form of shadowing of private guards and use of key informants. A single informant has played a critical role in the research project acting initially as a gatekeeper to the project as a whole and subsequently as an important ongoing source of information and updating. As this chapter will discuss, that individual's role in relation to the security firm has changed radically in the two year period of fieldwork and the implications of that change for the gathering of data will be analysed. It is ironic that in a quasi-policing research project the role of the informant should be so significant as this has real parallels for contemporary public policing. There has been an increasing focus in policing on the deployment of informants as a source of criminal intelligence and related attention to the 'handling' of informants (Maguire and John, 1995). In a similar vein this project has required cultivation of crucial informants (Hammersley and Atkinson, 1995) to maintain the flow of information regarding the operation of the security company.

The major focus of the chapter will be the strand of the research concerned with the culture of private policing and specifically the ethical issues which emerge from a heavy reliance on informants as a source of data. The fieldwork is still ongoing and the gathering of data remains an active task. Consequently many of the sensitivities and dilemmas regarding staying in and retaining access continue to be live.

Formulating the research problem

A key informant, for whom I shall use the pseudonym Martin, has played a critical role both in the initiation of the research project and as an ongoing source of data. Martin's initial relationship to the researcher was as a mature student in the social science department in which I lecture in criminology. Martin had completed a criminology diploma in the department in the mid 1980s and retained occasional contact with the staff group, usually by telephone, on crime related issues he had encountered in his local community. I was not a member of the lecturing staff when Martin was a student in the department. I was known to him as a member of the college staff with an interest in police research, having spoken to his diploma class regarding police related research with which I had then been involved. In mid 1996, he rang me to discuss a private security company that had begun operating near his home and with whom he had made contact.

The firm had been operating for several years, during which time they had been the subject of a BBC documentary but had recently been taken over by a new director who was a former employee of the company. The major focus of the work of the company was providing neighbourhood patrols for the residential area in which the director of the company lived. Residents in the area, which consisted primarily of private housing with some housing association provision, were canvassed and invited to join the private security scheme. Joining entailed paying a financial contribution of up to £2 per week to fund the running of the company. Martin was involved with the company on a voluntary basis, helping with paperwork and voluntarily accompanying the guards on neighbourhood patrols. Aware of my interest in the concept of private security, he offered to introduce me to the company director and facilitate any research that I might be interested in undertaking.

Martin adopted a pivotal role in the research project acting as a gatekeeper and introducing me to James (pseudonym), the company director. It was also evident at the first meeting with James and his staff that Martin had invested time before the face to face meeting in establishing my credentials as an experienced academic researcher with a track record in police research. He talked openly about the police research projects that he was aware I had been involved with and enquired about the personal well-being of senior academic colleagues. While we had not engineered a formal strategy, his enquiries at the first access meeting enabled me to demonstrate knowledge of key local police personnel, also known to James and to thereby substantiate my claim to be a credible police researcher who should be given access to his company.

Diverse agendas

In negotiating access to James' company it was evident that the three parties, James, Martin and myself all came with different agendas and investments in the outcomes of the research. James saw the academic links as raising the professional profile and image of the company. The firm was small scale, consisting of himself and four staff, one of which was his brother. It was also relatively local and parochial in its operations. The company operated from his home and covered the residential area in which he lived. He had plans to expand the company and saw an academic research input as supporting that expansion. He had no fixed ideas about how my research would be carried out, but his positive stance was reflected in the fact that his 'co-operation' with the research was prominently advertised at a very early stage in the newsletter regularly distributed to his customers. It was evident that my experience of police research and local knowledge was not perceived as in any way a threat, but rather a compliment to the quasi-policing nature of his organisation. Martin saw introducing me to the company as enhancing his own credibility and position. He came with some academic knowledge and expertise and took every opportunity to reinforce his own links with the university. He worked to convince James that my input as an independent evaluator of the operations of the company could only serve to enhance their commercial status. Following the maxim that all publicity is good publicity, there was never any suggestion from him or James that my research might reflect negatively on the company. My own agenda was that at an early stage I saw this research area as having potential as my doctoral thesis. I was personally committed to undertaking a PhD and a previous project had recently floundered, primarily on issues of access. While I saw real potential in this research topic, I elected to bide my time and observe how the research possibilities developed. Unlike Fountain's (1993) ethnography with drug dealers, I was not completely candid at the outset with either of my gatekeepers regarding my personal motivation for an interest in the research topic.

Research strategies

Having agreed access, the first stage to the research was a familiarisation with the working of the company. James' co-operation included an acceptance that I came with an open agenda on the exact form which the research would take. Gaining an understanding of the organisation of the company involved some perusal of paperwork and documentary evidence, including publicity materials, work logs and newsletters distributed to customers. Participant observation entailed accompanying the guards on night time patrols and joining James in his early evening walkabouts collecting payments from customers. During this period, I met key players in the company including James' wife who played a significant administrative role in the firm. An ongoing feature of this period was the continuing presence and influence of Martin. He was regularly present when face to face meetings took place and he and I had regular independent contact by telephone on how the research was progressing. His role evolved beyond that of gatekeeper to informant and the information he acquired and passed on to me was an important element in my understandings of the day to day running of the organisation. As an informant, Martin had been self selecting in promoting the project idea; his insider position within the company giving him access to a range of information which he was prepared to share with myself. This insider knowledge was important in researching a commercial company with an investment in putting a positive gloss on how well the firm was functioning.

Hammersley and Atkinson (1995, p.104) discuss the roles adopted by ethnographers as a continuum from complete participation to complete observation. My own role with the company laid major emphasis on observation. In the research setting I chose to cement early relationships with informants by means of direct participation and face to face encounters and subsequently to maintain such relationships by more sporadic contact, typically by telephone. My initial role in relation to the company and key informants evolved from participator to observer, with the time invested in

146

cultivating the informant facilitating the subsequent flow of information via more indirect means. This research strategy best fitted the objectives of the research which were to explore patterns of change over time in the operation of the private security company. I was not interested in a snapshot which an intensive period of fieldwork would have provided but rather the evolution of the company and its relationship to other key agencies over an extended period of time. To date access has been retained for a two year period, during which time a series of significant events have occurred in the development of the company and deployment of informants has proved an effective strategy in 'staying in'. Contact with both Martin and James has been retained throughout this period and at a later stage a further informant, Judy (pseudonym) was recruited whose knowledge related to expansion of the company into another locality. While the use of informants has proved an effective strategy for this project, this method is not without its potential pitfalls and dilemmas (Johnson, 1990) and the remainder of this chapter will deal with the problems encountered in this piece of work.

Problems in 'handling' informants

Checks on the validity of data

Fountain (1993, p.162) drawing on Burgess (1982) highlights the dangers of relying exclusively on informants' accounts and the potential for distortion. As informants' accounts provided a core element in the data collated regarding the operation of the security firm, alternative strategies by which accounts could be validated were particularly crucial. The three major informants held unique and distinct positions in relation to the company and while their perspective on events reflected that position, some checking out of their accounts against each others was feasible. On an insider/ outsider continuum, James, as the director of the company, was a clear insider whose representations were premised on that position. Martin's position bridged the insider/outsider role. As an interested volunteer, he was given access to important inside information but his affiliation to the company was not that of a paid employee and as such he was willing to divulge information that provided a more objective stance on how the business was progressing. As I will discuss below, Martin's position in the company shifted, becoming increasingly marginal as the research progressed, which impacted on the perspectives he was able to provide. In contrast, Judy's position was one of complete outsider. Her contribution became significant when the security company expanded into

147

her community and she adopted an oppositional position. Her interest reflected her position as an active neighbourhood watch co-ordinator with established links to the public police. She became an important source of information on how the public police viewed the infiltration of private groups into their patch. Each of the key informants regularly provided information reflecting their structural position in relation to the organisation, with the researcher positioned to check accounts against other core perspectives. The regularity of contacts, particularly with Martin, also allowed for a checking of internal consistencies in accounts given over time. During the two years of fieldwork Martin has typically spoken with me several times a week regarding how things are progressing with the company, increasing to several times a day at critical periods. As part of the cultivation of what I recognised to be important data I went out of my way to be available and receptive to such calls, even at those times when they felt intrusive and did not fit with my research timetable. While it was not feasible for me to be permanently in the field, I was alert to making myself as available as possible to informants. If I was really too busy to speak to my informants at the point when they called, I was conscientious about calling them back as soon as possible. I had an ansaphone available in my office and was equally assiduous about returning messages. Prioritising the maintenance of contact and availability to informants have proved important and effective strategies in maintaining the flow of information over an extended period of time. Other methods deployed in the research, alongside the informants' accounts, have also proved to be important means of validating such data. The perspectives provided by the neighbourhood survey and formal and informal interviews with the public police have supplemented in important ways the informants' accounts.

Shifting roles

A reliance on a small number of informants can be a dangerous strategy as changes in their status or position can directly impact on the researcher's access. My experience with this project is that Martin's position shifted substantially during the period of field work from insider gatekeeper to excluded outsider. This has been a gradual process but one which could have adversely affected researcher access. The changing attitude to Martin developed out of his perceived over identification with groups opposed to the expansion of the company. He developed his own links with Judy and neighbourhood watch groups which in James' eyes put in question his reliability and loyalty. As a consequence, in recent months his access to organisational information has been curtailed. His exclusion was confirmed

148

a few months ago when James rang me to provide the new phone number that the company were operating from and specifically requested that I did not share the number with Martin. At this point James was aware that I had continuing contact with Martin and his ostracising of him could have put my own access in jeopardy. This scenario was prevented by the time scale of events, with Martin's expulsion occurring some eighteen months into the fieldwork period. At this stage in fieldwork relations I had developed significant direct relationships with James and had moved well beyond using Martin as a go-between. The fact that I had had the opportunity to develop a direct role with the company prevented me being excluded with my personal gatekeeper and enabled me to retain access. Once Martin had been excluded, a strategic decision had to be made regarding retaining him as an informant. In practice, even as an outsider, he had important contributions to make regarding information he was able to share from significant others. The information he provided from groups in opposition to privatised security, including some public police officers, proved valuable. It was important however to understand the changing context of the data provided by a key informant (Hammersley and Atkinson, 1995).

Overt and covert roles

As Fountain (1993) acknowledges, frequently ethnographers are required to deal with the 'delicate combination of overt and covert roles' (Adler, 1985 p. 27) and my role as the researcher in this study was no exception. My decision to retain contact with Martin once he had forfeited his position in the security company was not something that I highlighted with James. While my own access had survived Martin's exclusion, I was aware that continuing contact with him was likely to be seen by James as threatening to the positive image of the company that he sought to convey. I was also aware of behaving covertly at an early stage in the project in 'selling' my original research idea to James and convincing him that I should be given access to his organisation. Supported by Martin my rationale for the research was an interest in evaluating the impact of private policing on the local community. While this is part of what the research is about and it is not untrue, it does not tell the complete story. Following Norris (1993 p.128) it provides a 'serviceable account' of what the research was about obscuring other more covert objectives. In practice, I was interested in the culture of private policing and how the occupational role compared with public police officers. I was interested in the viability of private security in residential areas as a commercial enterprise and the implications of such developments for the delivery of law and order. My cover story of researching the residents rather than the security company constructed the research role in a way that made it 'understandable and acceptable to the researched' (Norris, 1993, p.129).

Dangerous/ secret knowledge

As the period of fieldwork progressed and Martin's structural position in the company became more marginal, he increasingly provided me with confidential information which put in question the commercial viability of the business. As a researcher I was faced with a situation where key informants were providing markedly different constructions on how the company was developing. James' representation focused on what he perceived as positive developments, including the expansion of the business into new residential areas and his ability to move the business premises out of his home and into a commercial location. In contrast, Martin's accounts increasingly highlighted a range of problems which suggested that the future of the company might be in jeopardy, including problems regarding financial insecurities. While on the face of things it appeared that the company was expanding and transferring its location into commercial premises, there were ongoing cash flow problems with established clients. The image presented by Martin was much more one of financial instability and uncertainty. Much of the information provided by him was gleaned from his established contacts with the public police. From this source it became evident that there were a series of problematic issues in relation to the operations of the company. Martin indicated that there were problems regarding the adequacy of insurance cover with which the company were operating which involved external enquiries by trading standards officials. Questions were raised as to whether the company staff had criminal records and the related accuracy of publicity materials distributed by the firm. The public police had concerns about some of the operational methods being deployed, including allegedly listening in to police messages in order to arrive at incidents ahead of the police and, more seriously, encouraging young people to instigate disorder incidents as a means of encouraging residents to sign up for the private policing scheme. My own contacts with the police confirmed that the firm and its operations were the subject of close scrutiny and investigation. I became aware that some of the information that was being passed to me was unknown to the company and knowledge of it could have been valuable to the future survival of the firm. Martin, part of whose allegiance was to the success of the research project, became increasingly concerned that I complete my neighbourhood surveys before any official action was taken against the company. It was evident to me that on several fronts the company might face official action which would push it over the edge and out of business. The ethical dilemma for myself was that I was a party to such knowledge and was in a potentially exploitative position in not sharing such awareness with James. He had allowed me access to research his company and at the same time I was withholding information from him that might help him secure the future of the business, or at least protect himself from possible investigation. I was conscious that the covert activities and related knowledge that I had acquired placed in jeopardy the rapport I had established with the security company and the continuation of the fieldwork.

Dangers of over identification at the research site

The dilemmas for a researcher regarding covert activities and knowledge are intensified when there has been an extended period of fieldwork with a relatively few individuals. I have been in the field for two years on this project and have come to know the key players as individuals. Familiarisation with a small commercial company also involved direct relations with the wife and child of the company director and an awareness of the extent to which the success of the business was critical for the whole family. As the fieldwork progressed and particularly as the research revealed a range of problems in the operations of the company, I encountered increasing challenges to my construction of the research role as objective researcher. I was conscious of feelings of loyalty to the company and individuals connected to it and the risk that such a position would detract from the broader research perspective. Feelings of identification were premised on my level of knowledge of the research subjects and their accommodations to the project, including their ready acceptance that this would constitute my PhD, once this intention was revealed to them. Fountain (1993 p.165) recognises the related guilt which can emerge from the 'ethical compromises made by covert researchers' and the fieldwork relations of this project support that position.

In the context of the work as a whole, I was aware that over identification with the security company had to be avoided to protect other strands of the research, particularly work being undertaken with the police and the general community. Presentation of my research role to external audiences required an emphasis on the objectivity of my status to achieve the necessary access. There were real dangers in my being depicted as acting on behalf of the company, a factor which I was made aware of in the

151

early stages of negotiating my community research. I had attended a community meeting to inform them of my intention to do a household survey of members and non members of the private policing scheme. The group was made up of residents representing community groups and professionals from a range of agencies working in the locality. My rationale for attending was that this was a useful forum through which to inform the community about the research and to explain my presence approaching residents in the area. I was open to answering questions about the research, but had not anticipated the level of resistance that the project attracted from a key political figure attending the meeting. He fundamentally questioned the motivation for the research and was openly sceptical regarding the objectivity of the project. His direct questions as to who was funding the research were potentially seriously undermining in an open community meeting. Convincing key community players, both inside and outside that meeting, of the academic rigour of the project depended heavily on my being able to confirm the neutrality of the project and the lack of any allegiance to a particular interest group. In a project which sought to establish multiple access to a range of groups the separation of the researcher's interests from any particular group becomes highly significant. For this project that factor was also pertinent for the research components that involved the public police. The research was structured so that the majority of the work with the public police occurred toward the end of the fieldwork period. While informal contacts with the police have been ongoing, the formal interviews with senior police personnel were scheduled to follow the private police fieldwork and the neighbourhood surveys. It was felt that this would give the opportunity to test police responses to the results of the neighbourhood survey and the findings from fieldwork with the private police. This research schedule has been such that the researcher has in recent months negotiated a fine line between staying in and retaining access with the security company, while being perceived as a neutral academic in order to retain credibility with the police. At the same time the company, facing the commercial difficulties outlined above, has had an increasing investment in the outcomes of the neighbourhood survey as a core element in promoting a positive image of the business. Two years into the fieldwork the tensions in how the research role is constructed for diverse groups has increased.

Conclusion

At the time of writing, the research project is ongoing and field relations remain active with all three key informants and other personnel. The multi method approach has proved effective in uncovering important findings in an under-researched area of policing. The analysis of findings from the neighbourhood survey will be known in the next few months and as originally agreed will be shared with James, the company director. It remains in question whether the elements of the survey which reflect positively on an enhanced role for private policing will prove sufficient to ensure the survival of the business or whether the range of difficulties already encountered will force its demise. What is certain is that the issue of private policing is a significant one and as such it is likely to occupy an increasingly central position on the criminal justice agenda of the future. Evidence from this study would suggest that qualitative research methods will have a significant contribution to make in furthering academic scholarship in this area.

References

Adler, P.A. (1985) *Wheeling and Dealing: An Ethnography of an Upper-Level Drug Dealing and Smuggling Community,* Columbia University Press, Washington DC.

Bell, C. and Newby, H. (1977) *Doing Sociological Research,* Allen and Unwin, London.

Burgess, R.G. (1982) (ed) *Field Research: A Sourcebook and Field Manual,* Allen and Unwin, London.

Fountain, J. (1993) Dealing with Data in Hobbs, D. and May, T. (eds) *Interpreting the Field: Accounts of Ethnography,* Clarendon Press. Oxford.

Hammersley, M. and Atkinson, P. (1995) *Ethnography: Principles in Practice,* Tavistock, London.

Holdaway, S. (1983) *Inside the British Police,* Basil Blackwell, Oxford.

Johnson, J. (1990) *Selecting Ethnographic Informants,* Sage, London.

Johnston, L. (1992) *The ReBirth of Private Policing,* Routledge, London.

Loader, I. (1997) Thinking Normatively About Private Security, *Journal of Law and Society,* 24 (3).

Maguire, M. and John, T. (1995) *Intelligence, Surveillance and Informants: Integrated Approaches,* in Crime Detection and Prevention Series, Paper 64, Home Office, London.

Newburn, T. and Jones, T. (1998) *Private Security and Public Policing,* Clarendon Press, Oxford.

Norris, C (1993) Some Ethical Considerations on Field-Work with the Police in Hobbs, D. and May, T. (eds) *Interpreting the Field: Accounts of Ethnography,* Clarendon Press, Oxford.

Sheptycki, J. (1997) Insecurity, risk suppression and segregation: some reflections on policing in the transnational age, *Theoretical Criminology,* 1 (3).

Wakefield, A. (1997) Who Guards the Guards? Investigating an Unregulated Industry, unpublished conference paper, American Society of Criminology Meeting, November 1997.

Wilkie, R., Mair, C. and Ford, C. in Morgan, P. (1995) *Privatization and the Welfare State,* Dartmouth, London.

10 Organised Crime in Mexico

Alejandra Gomez-Cespedes

Based on ethnographic research in Mexico City, this chapter will examine how qualitative research methods grant the flexibility needed in order to conduct research on organised crime. The social and political context is indispensable to understanding the dynamics of organised crime within a country or region. In global terms, this context becomes useful when focusing upon similarities and differences of the phenomenon. Due to widespread corruption at political high levels and to the identity of actors who take part in organised crime dealings, this study has encountered extreme sensitive issues. I will discuss the serious implications attached to the study of organised crime in Mexico, not only for government authorities and journalists but also for anyone wishing to investigate the phenomenon thoroughly.

Introduction

Organised crime has been the generator of many myths and legends encompassing a world of enormous distortion, terror, opulence and scandal. Early interpretations of organised crime were concerned with the structure of criminal organisations in the United States, especially those of Italian origin (Cressey, 1969; Ianni and Reuss-Ianni, 1972; Abadinsky, 1981). Also, attention was given to the dynamics and constituent rules of such groups (Cressey, 1969; Maltz, 1976). However, with the emergence of a healthy scepticism about conventional views of crime, studies began to observe organised crime within the American political machine and law enforcement agencies (Chambliss, 1978; Block and Chambliss, 1981; Jenkins and Porter, 1987). Subsequently, emphasis shifted to the entrepreneurial side of the phenomenon (Reuter, 1984; Haller, 1990).

Most of today's debate surrounding organised crime derives mainly from the fact that there is not an agreed upon definition of the phenomenon

(Abadinsky, 1994; Albanese, 1996; Van Duyne, 1996 & 1997; Ruggiero, 1996; Hobbs, 1997; Nelken, 1997). However, there is a shared view that organised crime is an activity that conveys (goods, persons, animals or money) clandestinely across frontiers in order to avoid payment of custom duties or in contravention of legal prohibition. Nevertheless, although criminal cross-border trade should be considered an essential attribute of organised crime, it does not embrace the whole picture. In Mexico, for example, the Federal Organised Crime Law[1] stresses the types of activities that fall under the term 'organised crime' leaving out activities such as serious fraud, fencing, labour racketeering or toxic waste disposal. Equally important is the notion of organised crime as a continuous criminal industry. This concept (prevalent in Europe and useful for the purpose of this study) is evident in the definition given by the German Federal police.[2]

In order to have a genuine understanding of organised crime, one needs to ask how the social system of a region or country is organised so as to facilitate crime? In this context, it is important to note that the legitimate order will become the most important data to frame the analysis of criminal organisations for it is the legitimate opportunity structure which dictates the rules for the illegitimate opportunity structure (Cohen, 1977). Currently political discourses around the world agree that the threat which organised crime poses is its potential to penetrate political and financial systems and destroy them from within. Although this seems plausible, it is worth mentioning that the exploitation of the institutional order does not need an alien criminal penetration, for it can be criminally exploited by insiders (Cohen, 1977; Waller and Yasmann, 1997). In Mexico, when one analyses organised crime and the institutional bureaucratic corruption that has allowed prominent criminals (among which, 'narcotraficantes', kidnappers and corrupt bankers and politicians are only some examples) to flourish, it becomes apparent that the country's political, economic, security and law enforcement elites are fundamentally part of the problem.

Twenty years ago, Johnson (1978) argued that the Mexican political system, law enforcement agencies, security and intelligence bodies were the culture (as in bacteria) in which bureaucratic corruption and crime grew. Today, in an era in which organised crime is often the scapegoat for the nation's maladies, law enforcement agencies and intelligence services far from combating organised crime and corruption are often part of the problem. This is not only due to their (conscious or unconscious) recruitment of criminal elements and the use of crime as an instrument of state policy, but also due to the absence of a legal bureaucratic culture and a system of moral values.

156

Merton (1968) was the first to make the point that corruption could have both functional and dysfunctional effects for maintaining the social system. In Mexico, the problem of corruption is not new. In fact, it could be argued that corruption preceded the Republic (Bernecker, 1994). However, up until the early 1980s corruption had an integrating effect under the absolute power of one sole political party.[3] Prior to that, opposition and criticism were more like instances of treason and subversion, thereby attracting severe punishment (Bay, 1968; Johnson, 1978). Today, the PRI is losing its monopoly on political legitimacy and we see the arrival of more actors in the so-called democratic game. Those actors competing for the presidential election of the year 2000 are more worried about exposing the corruption and the traditional illegal practices (which have been the unwritten rules of the system) than about producing sound strategies aimed at developing a more accountable elite and ruling classes.

Similar to the Russian case (Waller and Yasmann, 1997) Mexican leaders have begun to agree that the greatest present threat to the security of the Mexican State is internal corruption and widespread organised crime. Ironically, organised crime has flourished within the vast state security agencies, those same organisations on which the Mexican government, the Mexican people and the United States foreign policy are relying upon to fight the problem. Nevertheless, it is certain that those agencies do have honest and capable professionals, as evidenced by those whose positions and lives have been sacrificed. However, the control of the security and intelligence services is not in the hands of these individuals and, without domestic political will and global pressure, they are unlikely to secure it in the short term.

Against enormous odds, the observer of organised crime in Mexico must question why is organised crime out of control? How is crime in general organised and how is it different from organised crime? How well equipped are the willing authorities to guide the country to a better life, assuming their endeavours can succeed? And what is the threshold at which criticism becomes an offence? These are the issues one must come to grips with to understand what is happening in Mexico towards the end of the 20th Century.

The research discussed in this chapter can broadly be separated into three chronological and geographical stages. The first stage refers to the early days of the project in which a great deal of secondary and empirical data were analysed. The findings of this stage conducted mainly in the United Kingdom shaped the second and third stages of the study. The second stage of the study was conducted in Mexico City. This stage was characterised by the application of ethnographic methods at two different settings, and the

157

use of formal and informal interviews. The third and last stage was carried out back in the United Kingdom and consisted of further interviews and the analysis of fieldnotes. This work, therefore, is the first academic attempt to explore the nature of organised crime in Mexico and to examine systematically and independently the outlook of various agents and conditions that affect, or are affected by, the phenomenon of organised crime. What follows is a consideration of the methodological issues that emerged throughout the research process.

Researching sensitive topics

Organised crime is a topic that most criminologists would regard as sensitive. Renzetti and Lee (1993, p. 5) suggest that

> a sensitive topic is one that potentially poses for those involved a substantial threat, the emergence of which renders problematic for the researcher and/or the researched the collection, holding, and/or dissemination of research data.

Although there are topics which are sensitive *per se,* much of the sensitive nature of a topic emerges from the relationship between the topic and the social context within which the research is conducted. According to Lee (1993), one can expect research to be threatening within three main realms: (i) when the study becomes an 'intrusive threat' to private, sacred or stressful areas; (ii) when the study involves data on deviance and social control that could incriminate or stigmatise the subjects of study and, (iii) when the study relates to controversial issues where the researcher impinges upon the interests of powerful people or organisations.

For a variety of reasons, the study of organised crime in Mexico encompasses all of these aspects of sensitivity. Lee (1993) suggested that when studying sensitive topics, participant observation and in-depth interviewing are the preferred methods of research. When the researcher has an overt identity, they can complement participant observation with in-depth formal or informal, unstructured or semi-structured interviews. According to Burgess (1984) these kind of interviews are perceived as 'conversations with a purpose'.

In fact, the use of ethnographic methods characterises most of the empirical research conducted on the study of contemporary organised crime and other sensitive topics. Due perhaps to the fact that the organised crime researcher is dependent on all sorts of opportunities granted by the police,

158

the Public Prosecution Office, governmental and financial institutions, and ultimately organised crime offenders, ethnographic methods grant the flexibility required for this particular kind of investigation (see for example Levi, 1981; Gambetta, 1993 and Passas and Nelken, 1993, for some early studies along these lines). This methodological approach has been used to study sensitive topics as diverse as drug trafficking (Adler and Adler 1980, 1982), long-firm fraud (Levi, 1981) and money laundering (Gold and Levi, 1994).

The value of ethnography

Ethnography focuses on being a participant observer in a group subjected to study, although contemporary ethnography uses a wide range of methods (Pearson, 1993). The ethnographer will get involved in a particular field in order to observe and record what is going on in that place. Thus, ethnography

> In its most characteristic form involves the ethnographer participating, overtly or covertly, in people's daily lives for an extended period of time, watching what happens, listening to what is said, asking questions - in fact collecting whatever data are available to throw light on the issues that are the focus of the research (Hammersley and Atkinson, 1995, p. 1).

Ethnography, like many other research strategies has many strengths but it also has potential weaknesses. Examples of the latter include unpredictability in the development of the project for many factors will interact to create unexpected situations. The inexperience of the ethnographer in an unfamiliar setting carries intrinsically the potential danger of missing significant evidence. However, as Levi (1981) said, sometimes 'the naive discover things the wise do not'. In the same vein, James Spradley mentioned that

> The more you know about a situation as an ordinary participant, the more difficult it is to study it as an ethnographer... It is no accident that ethnography was born and developed in the study of non-western cultures. The less familiar you are with a social situation, the more you are able to see the tacit cultural rules at work
>
> (Spradley, 1980, p.61-2).

159

Nevertheless, it must be borne in mind that participation depends largely on what the researcher is looking for: underlying rules or confidential data. In case of the latter, access to confidential data may be more available to an insider.

Although access and settings are important, the capacity for observation and/or participation depends greatly on the ethnographer's personality (Burawoy, et al., 1991; Vidich and Lyman, 1994). In most cases, ethnography is an individual experience that brings different problems to different people at different stages. Basically, one of the most serious limitations that ethnography poses is that it rarely can be replicated; not only because of the researcher's personality but also because of the diversity of factors that emerge after certain activities or inquiries (Allan and Skinner, 1993) or that emerge spontaneously in the natural process of a particular setting.

Nevertheless, ethnography emphasises the ways in which individuals and groups take for granted the rules according to which they operate. Ethnography constitutes a basic step for any in-depth investigation as it provides strong evidence of what people say, what people do and how they understand the way in which they structure their everyday lives. Moreover, it has been discussed that ethnography can generate good qualitative material of how offenders, victims and criminal justice officials perceive and experience crime. Indeed, ethnography grants the flexibility one needs in order to investigate sensitive topics.

Conducting the research

It became necessary to travel to Mexico in order to collect data from the place of origin. I chose Mexico City to conduct my study because most of the governmental, business and academic life of the nation is centralised there. Yet surprisingly, I found neither academic nor official data within the country. Contacts were made way in advance prior to the trip to Mexico and access to several government institutions was granted. However, when I arrived in Mexico, people I had contacted at the early stages of the project were no longer in their positions and I had to renegotiate access.

Fetterman (1991) says that the most salient attributes for successful fieldwork include curiosity, commitment to learning, patience, sincerity and honesty. Sarsby (1984) also maintained that skills in techniques were directly correlated to being in the right place at the right time. To say that successful events in the field result from elaborate planning and determination as much from a strike of good luck is in my view and experience a genuine statement.

The minute I walked into Federal Government Agency (FGA), I was forced to go through a process of security measures, which included use of a metal detector and a bag search. Soon after, I found myself before a front desk where a receptionist asked me who had I come to see. I told her I had come to see the head of FGA, and then she asked me if I had an appointment. 'No' I responded, 'I came to make the appointment myself.' She asked me for ID, picked up the telephone, called the head office and announced my visit. When she put the telephone down, she gave me a badge and a piece of paper that needed to be signed by the person I was going to meet. Then, she showed me the way and I went to the office of the head of FGA. When I arrived there, a secretary asked me further personal details which she entered into her computer. She told me I would not be able to speak to the head of FGA but that I could meet with his private secretary. Thus, after a few minutes, I had a meeting with that private secretary. I introduced myself, told him about my project and asked him if there was any chance of getting access to databases or people that worked with organised crime in Mexico. He told me that there was someone that could help me right there in FGA. However, he mentioned it would be very difficult for me to meet with this person as he was getting ready to leave the country within three days: he would be going on a three-month trip aimed at fortifying international co-operation in the fight against organised crime. Although the private secretary of the head of FGA knew this person was very busy, he gave him a call while I was sitting in front of him. Unfortunately, he could not find him but promised me that he would try to get in touch with him. Before leaving, I agreed to call the private secretary the following day in order to find out whether he had arranged an interview with the expert on organised crime or had someone else that could guide me in my study. That same evening I received a phone call from the private secretary of the head of FGA who told me the meeting had been arranged for the following morning.

The next day I met with the FGA's expert on organised crime. I introduced myself, talked about my project and asked him if he could help me. He told me that he was very interested but that I had a problem: 'he was leaving in two days so he would not be able to help me.' However, he asked me to come the following day so I could meet his staff. The day after, I was introduced to the whole staff, marking the beginning of a long and trustworthy relationship. When I think in retrospect about the access to this government agency I consider I was in the right place at the right time.

Many factors beyond my control interacted to make this a smooth entry into my fieldwork. First of all, people at the front desk never questioned the purpose of my visit. Secondly, the private secretary of the head of FGA not only contacted the expert but was also able to secure a meeting for me. Then, if I had delayed my visit a few days, I would not have been able to contact the expert who became my gatekeeper in Mexico. Perhaps if he had not left the country, he would not have advised his staff to grant me all their help while he was gone. I think my access was also facilitated by the fact that organised crime was a key issue at that time and legislative reforms were taking place.

It also paralleled a new and more open generation of politicians who were always willing to help. My name meant nothing to these people so I believe their co-operation derived from the fact that I started right at the top and in a centralised system like the Mexican political system. Subordinates rarely question the people who come to meet with 'el patron'. In fact, I was not familiar with the protocol of clientele networks which called for a gatekeeper that could grant you access to political figures at high levels. Luckily, I was naive enough to think that the only way to speak to senior politicians was person to person: it seemed logical and it worked.

My experience at FGA lasted eleven months. I went there twice or three times a week, depending on my interviews and examination of secondary sources. The staff always invited me to their discussion meetings and in fact, my views and opinions had considerable weight. On one occasion they called me to participate actively in the construction of an official report on casinos. On a different occasion, I conducted a long session on organised crime. They gave me books and we exchanged a lot of ideas, concepts and data. People used to come and go all the time, but it really did not matter who was there; they always made me feel part of the team. Although invariably I carried a notebook with me, I did not take notes while I was there - unless they gave me specific information. Following Levi (1981) it was not until I went back to my flat in the evenings that I recorded what I had observed and commented about it. Even when a tape-recorder had been accepted, information was so sensitive that it could fall into the wrong hands at some point. Thus, conversations held at FGA were not recorded. I learned the language of the people. I learned their habits, work patterns, leisure activities and their personal lives. Many times I accompanied them for lunch and at other times, we made specific appointments to meet for breakfast and then we went together to FGA. On several occasions, they gave me confidential documents and we shared long hours of work. At times, they asked me to write reports which I always enjoyed doing. There was only one time that I was not allowed to come into the office, because the staff were working with highly sensitive data. In fact, one of them told me that they did not want me to come in, not because they did not trust me, but because they were concerned about my personal security. At that time, a small group of the staff had long 'closed' sessions. Those sessions were very important because they demonstrated two of the most important characteristics of the group: cohesion and trust. In a government agency like FGA where information is always leaked, it was very interesting to observe that the purpose of those closed sessions was not known before the plan was put in action, that is, the dismissal of various FGA agents in connection with corruption and/or narcotics trade.

After this operation took place, the senior staff of FGA started getting death threats and there was an incident that created a very tense atmosphere. I stopped hanging around with them. However, I still went to visit them at FGA, less regularly than before. A few months after I returned to the United Kingdom, the head of FGA was dismissed and most of the staff team was disbanded.

At Mexico City university

At the same time I was conducting fieldwork at FGA, I registered in a Diploma on Policing Studies at a Mexico City university. Here, access was no problem for I could afford the tuition fees and had the right credentials. The diploma lasted nine months and it was only held on Wednesdays. The students attending the course were people working directly for the private or public security sectors. Again, nearly all of them were male. The overall substance of the course was not useful academically but at the same time it was helpful in my understanding of police cultures in Mexico.

Unquestionably, most of my learning derived from conversations with lecturers and people attending the course. Discussions in the lecture room were of enormous value in grasping different views of the police subculture. I recorded the lectures and consequently analysed the contents of the audiocassettes. Although we rarely addressed sensitive topics such as the dynamics of police deviance, the tapes compensated for the lack of (academic) information about the police in Mexico. In general, the relationship amongst the group was quite harmonious. Personally, I was able to establish good rapport with all my fellow classmates, as most of them were very kind people. In fact, I was very surprised when I later discovered that some of them had long records of corruption and deviance.

Interviews

I conducted both informal and formal interviews in both settings. Formal interviews were made with people I had never met before and that I had contacted over the telephone. As I did not know the people, I thought that a professional approach would give me the authenticity to convince people I was conducting a serious study for a doctoral degree. In the case of the informal interviews, they usually originated while doing participant observation when conversations turned toward my research topic. In doing interviews, it was found out that network or snowball sampling was the best way of gathering an appropriate sample (Lee, 1993). Network sampling consists of starting with an initial set of contacts and then being passed on by them to others, who in turn refer to others and so on (Burgess, 1992; Lee, 1993). However useful, bias is an almost inevitable characteristic of snowball samples (Lee, 1993; Renzetti and Lee, 1993). Rather than providing linkages to subjects whose views are different, networks tend to be homogeneous in their beliefs (Granovetter, 1973; Lee, 1993).

Informal interviews were unstructured, as much of the conversation was marked by the interviewee's views. Nevertheless, I observed that every time I showed interest in their conversations, respondents became more confident and I was able to obtain a series of deep insights into their way of life. Our conversations were of great value because they provided detailed data that matched with other materials.

In the case of formal interviews, these were framed in a semi-structured format with open-ended questions. This was done because I was not sure that I would have a second chance of meeting with the people and I needed to get as much information as I could in one session. Further in-depth questions arose from the responses given by the interviewee. Interviews took place in a variety of public and private places which depended largely on the choice of the interviewee. These locations largely comprised restaurants and their offices.

Every time I started an interview, I assured my interviewee about the intentions of my research. I told them I was doing an investigation for academic purposes. I told them I was a student at Cardiff University and that I was conducting fieldwork on organised crime. I further assured them that their identity would not be revealed unless they wanted me to do so. I observed, as a recurring pattern, that most interviewees agreed to disclose information provided I did not mention their names. Thus, once the confidentiality had been established, every effort was made to gain a rapport with the subjects. Although I always brought a notebook with me, I never took notes while the interview was taking place unless they gave me specific names of future contacts. I felt that the obvious presence of a notebook would inhibit their willingness to express their opinions. I usually wrote down the information minutes after coming out of the sessions. Rather than the location (office or restaurant), I noticed that people took their ease from my assurance of confidentiality. In other words, their willingness to talk became more apparent soon after I promised them I would not disclose their names, regardless of where the interview took place.

Leaving the field

By the time I returned to the United Kingdom the phenomenon of organised crime in Mexico was only starting to evoke response from the authorities and many events were happening very fast. Personally, I found it very difficult to evaluate events that were taking different shapes on different fronts and which at the time of my departure had not concluded. Legal hearings, police investigations and legislation reforms continue as I write. Analysis was delayed partly because I kept on gathering material on ongoing issues. Reading daily journals (usually on the Internet) kept myself attached to the field.

Reflections on the research process

The research methods worked very well in practice and access to research arenas was achieved with little difficulty. Having said that, reflection must be given to gender as a significant factor. Like Ackers (1993), being a young, single woman in predominantly male contexts may have had some favourable impact on the opportunities for access. Also, it probably facilitated rapport with the subjects in the way that my female status was perceived as non-threatening thereby, permitting me to ask, participate and observe without much reservation. To be unobtrusive while having access to all types of information was indeed very useful.

It has been documented (Gurney, 1991; Ackers, 1993) that women are vulnerable to instances of sexism, sexual hustling and sexual harassment in the field, especially in male-dominated settings. While it is true that my gender could have put me in a vulnerable position, in practice, I never experienced anything other than co-operation and kindness from both males and females. Surprisingly, the instances of harassment I became aware of were perpetrated against men in homosexual and heterosexual encounters.

As mentioned earlier, timing was very important. A new generation of politicians was in power. They did not feel responsible for the problems they were trying to solve so in a way we were learning and discovering things at the same time. Perhaps, their openness derived more from their being novices, rather than from their being overtly kind to researchers. Another important factor that facilitated access and trust, was the fact that I was conducting research for a British (as opposed as Mexican) university. This facilitated the ways in which I could address issues that were, or are, considered taboo in Mexican terms. I observed that 'foreigners' could be very critical of the system provided they did not express their criticism in Mexico. Perhaps, that is one of the reasons why most of the academic research on organised crime in Mexico has been conducted by academics in other countries. Unlike these academics, I had some advantages: I was not a foreigner and, I was not perceived as one. Furthermore, I had no cultural or language barriers.

It has been argued that research conducted on politically sensitive or deviant groups may carry reprisals from the people subjected to analysis, if they feel too much is revealed (see Parsa, 1989). Indeed, the political climate surrounding this research makes it highly sensitive. Also, this study has unearthed dormant data and thus, can cause political discomfort. Before leaving Mexico, I was strongly advised to censor my findings. However, I felt compelled to provide an uncensored account. Self-censorship poses potential costs that cannot be overlooked. We lose relevant data that could lead to a better understanding of a phenomenon and if social problems go unreported, society misses an opportunity to do something about it. This work constitutes the first step in alerting society that the development or inhibition of organised crime in Mexico is concentrated within the elite political, economic and law enforcement structures and it is in that sphere that one must focus rather than looking for alien scapegoats elsewhere.

Mexico's democracy once seemed like an oasis amidst the desert of Latin American dictatorships. Abroad, many intellectuals and public relations firms reinforced Mexico's benign image. However, for many Mexicans, this oasis of democracy was a frustrating mirage. Conditions were not as they appeared from abroad. For those without privileged protection from the arbitrary exercise of government authority, life was very harsh. The glowing image of Mexico's political stability concealed a more disturbing reality. In a country where corrupt and criminal alliances are integrated all along the political and economic chains, promoting academic research on criminological and policing issues becomes a threat to deep and powerful interests. The Mexican system demands urgent changes within its criminal justice system and this in its turn, demands academic evaluation. However, true reforms only come when attitudes and practices change and when professionalism is enhanced. By contrast, in censoring academic studies Mexicans lose the opportunity to correct their own vices. It can only be hoped that future conditions allow Mexican academics to approach issues of deviance and social control in a more open and critical way.

Notes

1. Organised crime consists of three or more persons who agree to engage or engage in a permanent or continuous way on activities which, each or together have the purpose of committing the following offences: (1) terrorism, (2) offences against health, (3) counterfeiting and forgery, (4) operations with the proceeds of crime, (5) gathering and trafficking of weapons, (6) trafficking of immigrants, (7) trafficking of organs, (8) robbery, (9) kidnapping, (10) trafficking of children and, (11) auto-theft (Ley Federal contra la Delincuencia Organizada, Secretaria de Gobernacion, 1996).

2. Organised crime is the planned violation of the law for profit or to acquire power, which offences are each, or together, of a major significance, and are carried out by more than two participants who cooperate within a division of labour for a long or undetermined timespan using (a) commercial or commercial-like structures, or (b) violence or other means of intimidation, or (c) influence on politics, media, public administration, justice and legitimate economy (Küster, 1991 in Van Duyne, 1997).

3. The Institutional Revolutionary Party (PRI) has won presidential elections since 1929.

References

Abadinsky, H. (1981) The Mafia in America: An Oral History, Praeger, New York.
Abadinsky, H. (1994) Organized Crime, 4th ed., Nelson-Hall Publishers, Chicago.
Ackers, H. L. (1993), 'Racism, Sexuality, and the Process of Ethnographic Research', in Hobbs, D. and May, T. (eds) Interpreting the Field: Accounts of Ethnography, Clarendon Press, Oxford.

Adler, P.A. and Adler, P. (1980) 'The Irony of the Secrecy in the Drug World', *Urban Life*, 8, pp.447-465.

Allan, G. And Skinner, C. (eds) (1993) *Handbook for Research Students in the Social Sciences*, Reprint, The Falmer Press, London.

Albanese, J. (1996) *Organized Crime in America*, 3rd ed., Anderson, Cincinnati, OH.

Article 19 (1989) *In the Shadow of Buendia: The Mass Media and Censorship in Mexico*, Article 19, London.

Bay, C. (1968) *The Structure of Freedom*, Atheneum, New York.

Bernecker, W.L. (1994), *Contrabando: Ilegalidad y Corrupcion en el Mexico del Siglo XIX*, trans. Manuel Emilio Waelti, Universidad Iberoamericana, Mexico, DF.

Block, A.A. and Chambliss, W. J. (1981) *Organizing Crime*, Elsevier, New York.

Burawoy, M., et al. (1991) *Ethnography Unbound: Power and Resistance in the Modern Metropolis*, University of California Press, Berkley.

Burgess, R.G. (1984) *In the Field: An Introduction to Field Research*, Contemporary Social Research Series, 8, Allen & Unwin, London.

Burgess, R.G. (ed) (1992) *Learning About Fieldwork, Studies in Qualitative Methodology*, 3, Jai Press, Inc, Greenwich.

Chamblis, W. J. (1978) *On the Take: From Petty Crooks to Presidents*, Indiana University Press, Bloomington.

Cohen, A. K. (1977) 'The Concept of Criminal Organization', *The British Journal of Criminology*, 17 (2), pp.97-111.

Cressey, D.R. (1969) *Theft of the Nation*, Harper and Row, New York.

Fetterman, D.M. (1991) 'A Walk Through the Wilderness: Learning to Find Your Way', in Shaffir, W.B. and Stebbins, R.A. (eds), *Experiencing Fieldwork: An Inside View of Qualitative Research*, Sage, Newbury Park.

Gambetta, D. (1993) *The Sicilian Mafia: The Business of Private Protection*, Harvard University Press, Cambridge, Massachusetts.

Gold, M. and Levi, M. (1994) *Money Laundering in the UK: An Appraisal of Suspicion-Based Reporting*, The Police Foundation, Cardiff.

Granovetter, M.S. (1973) 'The Strength of Weak Ties', *American Journal of Sociology*, 78 (6), pp.1360-1380.

Gurney, J.N. (1991) 'Female Researchers in Male-Dominated Settings,' in Shaffir, W.B. and Stebbins, R.A. (eds) *Experiencing Fieldwork: An Inside View of Qualitative Research*, Sage, Newbury Park.

Haller, M. H. (1990) 'Illegal Enterprise: A Theoretical and Historical Interpretation, *Criminology*, 28, pp.207-235.

Hammersley, M. and Atkinson, P. (1995) *Ethnography,* 2nd. ed. Routledge, London.

Hobbs, D. (1997) 'Criminal Collaboration: Youth Gangs, Subcultures, Professional Criminals, and Organized Crime' in Maguire, M., Morgan, R. and Reiner, R. (eds) *The Oxford Handbook of Criminology,* Oxford University Press, Oxford.

Ianni, F. A. and Reuss-Ianni, E. R. (1972) *A Family Business: Kinship and Social Control in Organised Crime,* Russell Sage, New York.

Jenkins, P. and Porter, G. (1987) 'The Politics and Mythology of Organized Crime: A Philadelphia Case Study', *Journal of Criminal Justice,* 15, pp.473-484.

Johnson, K. F. (1978) *Mexican Democracy: A Critical View,* Rev. ed., Praeger, New York.

Lee, R.M. (1993) *Doing Research on Sensitive Topics,* Sage, London.

Levi, M. (1981) *The Phantom Capitalists: The Organisation and Control of Long-Firm Fraud,* Heinemann, London.

Maguire, M., Morgan.R., Reiner, R. (eds) (1997) *The Oxford Handbook of Criminology,* Oxford University Press, Oxford.

Maltz, M. D. (1976) 'On Defining Organised Crime: The Development of a Definition and a Typology', Crime and Delinquency, 22, pp.338-346.

Merton, R. (1968) *Social Theory and Social Structure,* Rev. ed., Free Press, New York.

Nelken, D. (1997) 'White-Collar Crime', in Maguire, M., Morgan, R. and Reiner, R. (eds) *The Oxford Handbook of Criminology,* Oxford University Press, Oxford.

Parsa, M. (1989) *Social Origins of the Iranian Revolution,* Rutgers University Press, New Brunswick, NJ.

Passas, N. and Nelken, D. (1993) 'The Thin Line Between Legitimate and Criminal Enterprises: Subsidy Frauds in the European Community,' *Crime Law and Social Change,* 19, pp.223-243.

Pearson, G. (1993) 'Talking a Good Fight: Authenticity and Distance in the Ethnographer's Craft', in Hobbs, D. and May, T (eds), *Interpreting the Field: Accounts of Ethnography,* Oxford University Press, Oxford.

Renzetti, C.M. and Lee, R.M. (eds) (1993) *Researching Sensitive Topics,* Sage, Newbury Park.

Reuter, P. (1984) *Disorganized Crime,* Cambridge, Massachusetts: MIT Press.

Ruggiero, V. (1996) *Organized and Corporate Crime in Europe: Offers that Can't Be Refused,* Dartmouth, Aldershot.

Sarsby, J. (1984) 'The Fieldwork Experience', in Ellen, R.F. (ed), *Ethnographic Research: A Guide to General Conduct*, ASA Research Methods in Social Anthropology, 1, Academic Press, London.

Spradley, J.P. (1980) *Participant Observation*, Holt, Rinehart and Winston, New York.

Van Duyne, P. C. (1996) 'The Phantom and Threat of Organized Crime', *Crime Law and Social Change*, 24 (3), pp.341-377.

Van Duyne, P. C. (1997) 'Organized Crime, Corruption and Power', *Crime Law and Social Change*, 26 (4), pp.201-238.

Vidich, A.J. and Lyman, S.M. (1994) 'Qualitative Methods: Their History in Sociology and Anthropology', in Denzin, N.K. and Lincoln, Y.S. (eds) *Handbook of Qualitative Research*, Sage, Thousand Oaks.

Waller, J. M. and Yasmann, V. J. (1997) 'Russia's Great Criminal Revolution,' in Ryan, P. J. and Rush, G. E. (eds), *Understanding Organized Crime in Global Perspective,* A Reader, Sage, Thousand Oaks, CA.

11 The social construction of fraud, trust, abuse and the private victim

Andy Pithouse

Introduction

Fraud crime hinges on the careful and illicit manipulation of the symbolic. Hence, this chapter will explore fraud as a social construction and in doing so will illustrate how qualitative methodology rooted in phenomenology is particularly suited to the study of this crime. Brief examples will be given of the experience of private citizen victims at the hands of fraudsters who use interpersonal skills, relationships and material artefacts to gain and then breach the trust of private citizens (for a more extensive account of the vast range of fraud activity and the various ingenious methods deployed to fleece individual citizens and organisations, see Punch, 1996). By using and abusing the cues and gestures of expected interaction, fraud crime does not simply injure the victim but damages the very fabric of the everyday world, which is based upon our assumption that people and events are generally what they appear to be. It is here that fraud becomes a unique and wholly appropriate topic for qualitative research, as it is this methodology that is best suited to grasp the subtle world of identity, meaning and process which fraudsters bring to a more self conscious level in order to exploit the motives and interests of others. This chapter will therefore attempt to grasp fraud crime through the generalising medium of the phenomenal and in doing so will locate its special character around the corruption of trust. First, the notion of trust will be outlined as an ethical and practical imperative of social and economic activity. Secondly we introduce trust in relation to a constructivist methodology. Thirdly, we consider the methods most appropriate to exploring fraud crime with private citizen victims and lastly we provide extracts from interviews to illuminate the ways in which fraud crime injures the trust and the self-esteem of victims.

Trust abuse and the victim of fraud

Trust is not simply an imperative of efficient commercial dealings or civilised sociation but is a diffuse aspect of community which itself provides the shared ethical habits or social capital that condition our propensity for sociability - for engaging with others in new associations or ventures (see Good, 1988). As the economist Fukuyama notes (1995 p.321-336), the relationship between social capital and economic performance is indirect if not indeterminate but a failure to recognise its significance may have far reaching consequences, particularly in those advanced economies where the social 'glue' of group association in all its manifestations weakens as more privatised and individualised life styles and interests predominate. In such a scenario, fraud would appear to be a particularly damaging crime in both its economic and social impact, even more so in those societies where social capital is already attenuated by a decline in communal opportunities to affirm or create the virtues of interdependence and shared values. If, as Fukuyama claims (1995, p.362), the key problems facing advanced economies are no longer ideological or institutional but the 'preservation and accumulation of social capital' - then the question of fraud and its unique relation to trust violation becomes a topic of concern that needs to be explored beyond its usual criminological confines.

The social significance of fraud lies in the violation of trust and the manipulation of people to make them believe something that is not true and thereby act in ways other than they would have, had they not been deceived. In this sense, fraud has its roots in the nature of the human psyche and cannot be regarded as some special technological crime of a modern economy. It is as old as human sociation itself in that deception and the lie have always been an available resource for every social actor (Bok, 1978). As argued here, fraud's social dimension is the exploitation of the symbolising resources we all draw upon to construct and sustain meanings in which we and others can believe. For most of us, commerce entails some degree of trust in the appearance of people and events, and it is the injury of this trust that marks out the distinctive social and psychological effects of this crime on both victim and society (see Dasgupta, 1988; Eisenstadt and Roniger, 1984; Rutter, 1980).

The social impact of fraud is not simply at the level of a theft or artful conduct: it has a more complex effect in the way in which, unlike other crimes, it engages the victim's co-operation by wilful manipulation of the symbols we all use to construct meaning in our day to day lives. Here, the victim is not just conned into participating in his or her own demise - however bad or unfortunate that may be - but also learns that the world is

172

no longer quite so believable as before. Of course, to the extent that s/he is aware that a fraud has occurred, the victim may have had a relatively painless but salutary experience, or may heedlessly continue to believe that this is the best of all possible worlds: that it is not may be discerned in the growth of UK fraud crime (see Levi and Pithouse, 1999) that now invites a growing social science interest, albeit, from a relatively small number of academics (Punch, 1996 p.74).

Fraud crime often calls for determined forensic examination in order to map out the complicated and uncertain route of some deception. Likewise, the victim often appears a shifting and contingent identity. Also, attributing a victim status in the sense of experiencing a personal and distressing event is clearly problematic in the context of an organisation. This is not to suggest that organisations and their members do not suffer significant 'pain' when fraud results in financial losses, unemployment or business failure. Whether fraud is a 'hit and run' event or an elaborate deception established over time, there is in both instances a 'process'. That is, the victim travels through the discovery, investigation and - perhaps - prosecution and sentencing of the fraudster. Fraud in this sense is not simply a criminal act, rather it signals the existence of some relationship into which the victim is drawn (see Titus, Heinzelmann and Boyle, 1995 p.63) and which frequently shifts the victim's perception of him/herself, of the fraudulent act and of the judicial system (Walsh and Schram, 1980). Attempts to conceptualise the victim identity as an abstract and 'typical' category are unlikely to reveal the dynamic career of events that occur between fraudster, victim and members of the justice system, and which calls for the careful selection of methodology and method, it is towards the former that we now turn.

Social construction and trust

While trust was rarely a core concern of the founders of sociology, the question of social order and its creation was a central topic (Eisenstadt and Roniger, 1984 pp.29-31). It was not until the emergence of a more phenomenological sociology, that took as its project the construction of meanings through symbolic interaction, that we have been able to conceive of trust as a generic property of our daily social encounters. Trust has as its dynamic aspect that it is constructed and understood within our available symbolising capacities. It is in the very arena of daily interaction and communication that we express our identities, our interests and our intentions. Here exist the resources at the disposal of all of us to reveal or

173

disguise our purpose at hand. Fraud in this sense is but a perverse manipulation of the reality we all construct in our everyday social world. Fraud is the illicit use of the symbolising resources (language and artefacts) we all rely upon to make sense of the world. As Becker (1972, p.100) notes '[t]he proper word or phrase, properly delivered, is the highest attainment of human interpersonal power'. How then do we routinely ensure that the world is as it appears to be in our encounters with others, given this ever-present potential for actors to dissemble and deceive?

This question has been at the centre of Goffman's (1967) dramaturgical analysis of the self in interaction. His work on the 'ceremony of the self' looks at the way we all trust our 'face' in our dealings with others. That is, we engage with others in the expectation that we will be generally treated with consideration and we trust people will conform to the social conventions that help construct our interaction. For example, we trust that the other will not break the tacit rules of expected performances by openly challenging what we believe are shared assumptions and views about the business at hand (see Garfinkel, 1967). In short, we sustain predictable interaction with all manner of others by necessarily believing in the performance presented to us providing that performance is reasonably competent. We may of course search for evidence of authenticity in a performance but we can never 'know' the other in some absolute sense. We can only assess the motivational sincerity of the other in the clues and cues they provide within the encounter. As Goffman notes, we are for the most part skilled performers and can often spot the insincere in others. We too are skilled at withholding our most heart-felt opinions in order to bring off an orderly and competent performance. But it is because we necessarily engage with others in the absence of reciprocal knowledge, without knowing for certain how things will proceed for us, that we all trust that the other will perform within tolerable limits, but broadly as expected. For Goffman the most believable performances are those that most affect the credulity of others and these typically occur when the performer takes him or herself seriously and is able to demonstrate this signal of authenticity. It is precisely this capacity to provide such a competent performance that makes the impostor so powerful. Here, victims are injured not merely to the extent of any specific losses but also because their capacity to interact is reduced by the fact that they can no longer assume the moral connection between appearance and intent.

Trust, as described in the context of a formalist and phenomenological sociology, situates the concept in the crucial currents of self, identity, and performance that are accomplished in conditions whereby knowledge is always partial, if not in error. Fraud, as an act that usurps these conditions, does so because it manipulates misleadingly the symbolising tools we use to make the world intelligible, and in doing so, it strikes as deep and insidious a blow to the individual and society as any other crime. The idea that trust underpins a social and moral order - in that we assume its place in the performance of others and in the assumptions we make about an uncertain world - is a crucial element in grasping the impact of fraud crime. From this theoretical position we now consider the selection of appropriate methods in relation to researching fraud victims and their sometimes very painful experience of trust violation.

Researching the fraud victim

Trust is a central theme of our everyday social, emotional and economic lives, and this holds true for the social research act. Enquiry into the motives and assumptions of people via qualitative methods, for example, observation and interview, depends in significant part upon the trust that is engendered between researcher and researched. Trust in this context may flow from many sources other than the deployment of ethical and effective methods of enquiry. Here, social ascription with regard to gender, race, ethnicity, age, class, status group and so forth will inevitably influence the research encounter, thus participants may well place more 'trust' in a researcher who presents 'as one of us'. Such congruence between identities in a research encounter may well provide a useful initial edge but cannot be assumed to be a sufficient basis upon which a research relationship is built. There are other complex aspects that will intrude, for example, respondents may be unlikely to confide with anyone over intensely personal matters unless they feel confident that they will not be put at risk in some way by disclosing sensitive issues. Interestingly, few contemporary research methods texts devote much space to trust in this context and tend to assume that it will arise within the ethical and technical conventions of research methods themselves, Indeed, the concern is typically more with the degree of trust that can be placed in the validity and reliability of instruments than in the process of a research encounter whereby participants evolve a measure of reliance on the integrity of the event as safe and non prejudicial.

However, there are likely to be contexts whereby some respondents will perceive risk when they are asked to disclose material that may directly or implicitly confer some negative status upon themselves. This is likely to occur in relation to crime victims who may sometimes cast themselves, or be viewed by others, as in some way responsible for inviting the harm done to them. This of course may or may not be true, but in any event a sense of stigma can attach to the victim experience. This is by no means unusual for private citizen fraud victims who may come to see themselves and / or assume others see them as somehow socially incompetent for being duped in some way. In circumstances such as these, the researcher has to be especially sensitive, empathic and non judgemental in order to elicit a trusting encounter where people will share their experience and rehearse the events leading to what is not only a financial harm, but a sense of status injury too.

Choosing the method

The 'long interview' (McCracken, 1988) was chosen as the most appropriate method to allow both viewer and respondent time to examine in depth the activities, meanings, relationships, settings and participants surrounding (a) the events leading up to a fraud against a private victim (b) the discovery of loss and its legal aftermath (c) the victim's consequent view of the perpetrator and the fraudulent act (d) their own participation in the fraud process and (e) the way the fraud had impacted upon them economically and socially. The research design allowed time for only one lengthy interview and it was decided to deploy a semi structured format that would facilitate elaboration and exploration but offer some structure of comparability (see Jones, 1996 p.161). An opportunity sample of private victims identified from recent fraud cases at a major Crown Court were contacted by letter which produced a positive response from twenty five individuals who indicated their willingness to be interviewed at their own homes (a full account of this research is contained in Levi and Pithouse 1999).

The study followed the guidance of McCracken (1988) who in describing the 'long interview' points to the way in which this broad, less bounded approach allows the respondent freedom to answer fully within their own frames of reference. Such an approach, as we shall see below, yielded illuminating material about the underlying assumptions or 'rules' (see Cicourel, 1964 pp.206-7) by which people socially organise their lives and the implicit but sometimes uncertain role of trust within this. It was of course not possible to 'observe' the events leading up to the fraud or the reaction of the victims, nor were there opportunities to interview other key participants who were involved in the fraud. Hence it was not possible to validate the views of the respondents through triangulation of methods (Denzin, 1970; Silverman, 1993). Thus while methodological pluralism (Miller and Dingwall, 1997) can be seen as the ideal approach to social

176

research, it was not possible to combine methods to any great extent in this small exploratory study. However, secondary data such as court records of the offence and witness statements were useful as a benchmark against which to examine any changes in perception and interpretation of events arising in victim interviews.

In searching out the fraud victim career, it has to be remembered that qualitative interviews do not simply facilitate some 'objective' recall. Rather the interview is implicated in the construction of meanings that lie within the victim experience. Meaning is therefore assembled in the interview process and not simply garnered by questioning (Silverman, 1993). Participants in the interview were not just containers of knowledge but collaborators in the constitution of knowledge and meaning (Holstein, Gubrium and Jaber, 1995). Thus both interviewer and interviewee become instruments of enquiry. The interviews were conducted in light of the advice, skills and problems noted in qualitative research methods texts and took note of linguistic and para-linguistic dynamics (see Hammersely and Atkinson, 1993). It must be re-emphasised that the interview is itself a social event, a temporal act existing in time and place and does not reveal invariant properties of a social world. Nor is there an invariant correlation between the asking of questions and the giving of information. Both the perceptions of interviewer and interviewee about the other will influence their reactions to the event. Inevitably, the researcher faces the same problem as any member of a social setting. That is, the sharing of sensitive information will crucially depend upon the ability to be accepted and trusted.

What follows now are accounts not so much of fraud as some discrete criminal event but of the ways in which victims have constructed a set of understandings in which to view themselves both before and after the fraud. These typically show a shift in perception about themselves as people who became not only financially worse off but also suffered injury to their own self conception as capable and competent social actors. Such personal disclosures are unlikely to be offered via a formal survey instrument or narrowly cast questionnaire (both appropriate for other forms of enquiry). Thus, for the discovery of more intimate experience and for gaining the trust of those for whom trust has been recently abused, the qualitative 'long interview', which allows both interview and interviewee time to establish themselves as genuine co-particpants in an exploration of meaning, proved in this instance to be the ideal method.

The private citizen as victim of fraud

> Well you do feel embarrassed about it because you feel, well me, I am such a clever person, I rate myself as a fairly wide boy, street-wise, and I sit back here and as I'm talking I'm smiling to myself. Even now I can get 'done', you know what I mean....

This extract from an interview with a middle aged couple who had bought a car that did not belong to the vendor reflects a typical response from victims. That is, a sense of shame, incredulity, and as shown later, a determination to remedy their injury. Most of the fraud victims interviewed were typically involved, albeit briefly, in face to face contact with the perpetrator and had placed their faith in the honest intentions of the wrongdoer. Most frauds were around the sale of goods or services and for relatively small amounts, but large enough for some victims on modest or fixed incomes. Most victims reported placing their trust in the fraudster having been convinced, or convincing themselves, of the authentic purpose of the business at hand. It was this abuse of trust that induced a sense of anger, guilt in some instances, and an injured sense of self esteem that warranted some response by the victims towards the fraudster - however unlikely this was to resolve their difficulties.

One middle-aged couple on fixed disability incomes were defrauded by a caller posing as the provider of cut-price coal. As days went by, it became gradually apparent that they were unlikely to see the caller, their cash or the coal. They did not tell the police immediately due to a sense of embarrassment and the feeling they were partly to blame for their losses - and might be seen as such by the authorities:

> Well you feel silly don't you, gullible. All for that silly old trick. You see it, you read about it, and then you go and do the same old thing! I was a little bit suspicious, but I thought, oh well, he looks all right, give him the money, that's what it boiled down to.

Likewise, a young female victim described how she met a young man in a pub who claimed he was a car salesman and could get a good price for her old car. She gave him the car and the documents and anticipated about £300 from a sale, less commission. She did not see the man or the car again until the case came to court:

I suppose I'm not as naïve any more now. I've learnt a lesson. ...I mean I believed him, he was a car dealer, I would never do that again... It was my fault in a way because I shouldn't have been so gullible.

Similarly, with a family who had lost over £200,000 to a banker friend in whom they had every confidence, it was still the case that self-recrimination featured prominently in the initial victim experience:

...at first my brother blamed himself...we sort of said to him - look it's not your fault, it could have happened to anyone... don't take this personally, it's nothing to do with you: just look at the trail of people who have been fooled.

During interviews victims sought to establish early on in their discussion some rationale for what they believed would be seen by significant others as their naïve or gullible conduct. For example, one victim who bought a car that was later repossessed by its rightful owner said:

I got the log book and got a receipt. I insured it, taxed it, what more could I do?

The couple who gave their money to a fraudster coal man who failed to deliver said:

He was very nice, very persuasive, dressed tidy, said that a girl up here he knew had been buying coal off him for ages...

The young female victim who gave her car and documents to the bogus car dealer believed she had taken some rudimentary precautions to check his claims:

He said he was a car dealer...took me to his parents house... he operated the business from the house...it all seemed above board...

The family from whom a close banker friend had stolen their savings of over £200,000 believed they could not have anticipated such an event:

He was a personal friend of the family, a friend of my elder brother, he'd known my family for over 20 years, possibly longer...

Feelings of self-reproach together with some concern for justifying their actions featured in all interviews with victims. Annoyance with themselves was matched with anger for the fraudster. This was not impotent rage but an anger associated with action of some kind. None of the victims were passive in the sense that they quietly accepted their plight and left matters to the authorities. Many sought to resolve things by attempting to make contact with the fraudster in order to seek recompense. For example, the couple who bought a stolen car made their own enquiries into the identity of the fraudster and they discovered where he went in his leisure time and went looking for him. The couple met a friend of the fraudster with whom they left the following message:

> I said 'I know you know him so you give him a message', I said 'I'll cut his legs off, I'll kill him stone dead', I said 'he done me for £2,300 besides God knows how many others...'

The fraudster got the message and was not seen again until the trial; the money lost on the car was never seen again. Similarly, the husband of the couple who lost out to the coal fraudster stated:

> He (fraudster) said he lived up on the housing estate... No one up there knew him. He told me the street he lived in, I didn't know the people there but I asked a few people if they'd seen him, I went to the address he gave and they didn't know the bloke, never heard of him, so I asked a few people - nobody had seen him.

The possibility of some other redress apart from money-back was also available to the young woman who had given her car to a bogus car dealer to sell on her behalf.

> Well a few boys I know - well I think they're nice - they offered to go down there and beat him up. I declined that offer. I didn't think that was going to solve anything.

For the family who lost over £200,000 to a banker-friend, there was no reluctance on the part of the young men of the family to visit the home of the family friend and have it out with him.

> ...we tried as best we could to de-emotionalise the situation. He came down pretty dishevelled looking. He'd been to London he'd been fired (by the bank) the same day. And we confronted him with it...and he just very coldly, no emotion at all, I suppose he must have been drained by then, told us basically the same story...that took about 45 minutes and we just left the house. There was nothing else we could do...

Throughout many of the interviews a sense of 'unfinished business' permeated the accounts of victims. This seemed largely due to the personal and painful sense of deception experienced by the victims. The fraudster must after all meet and then deceive his or her victim. It is this construction of a relationship abused that seems to deeply rankle the victim and create their ambivalent feelings of self-blame and anger against the fraudster. In the above examples the fraudsters were 'local' and were known to live nearby. In some instances the fraudster was seen again by the victim 'on the street', before and after appearing in court. In this context, fraud does seem to evince a relationship that is not likely to exist in the usual run of opportunistic street crime - as the following extracts reveal. For most respondents fraud was a personal affair; many attempted to describe a feeling of both being robbed and of giving their money away. It is this notion of theft through artful persuasion, of having been almost 'negotiated' out of one's property that gives the victim a feeling that they could somehow 'negotiate' back their losses or at least have the last word if they could meet the fraudster again. For example, the young woman who had lost her car to the young fraudster who had promised to sell it for her, met the young man on a few occasions before finally going to the police. Even after the court hearing and the fraudster's imprisonment, the young woman met him again some time after his release and once again sought some satisfaction:

> ...he was laughing. He said hello and I said 'what are you doing out?' He said 'I'm free now', or something along those lines, and I said 'I suppose you're going straight' and he said 'no I'm out to carry on!' I was quite cutting in my remarks but you'd never get your money back because he'd never get a job where he was on PAYE so you'd never get your money back.

The middle-aged couple who lost their money to a bogus coal-dealer had a similar experience. The female victim saw the fraudster in a local supermarket some weeks after his court appearance:

> I went down the supermarket and he was standing right by the door...you could have called him 'thief' but I don't suppose it would have done much good because he's conned a lot of people, he's not greatly concerned about his reputation. And I think if he mugged me or used physical violence I wouldn't have gone to him, but because he only defrauded me I felt as if I could speak to him. I felt I could have done a deal with him of some sort, I don't know why. He could pay me a pound or anything. I missed my chance and there you are.

Likewise, the couple who had lost over £2000 by buying a stolen car had managed to obtain the fraudster's address from a contact

> ...between you and me (the contact) told me where he was living but they said there's nothing you can do about it...I went up to his house and parked outside just to catch an eye of him. He had a big house but it belonged to the Bank, he got chucked out of that as well. He's done everybody, he never left a stone unturned!

Conclusion

The above selected extracts from qualitative long interviews suggest that the fraud victim responds to a temporal and interactive encounter with the fraudster that is likely to be different from the experiences of the ordinary street-crime victim. This stems most pertinently from the nature of 'doing' fraud as instanced here, that is, using manipulative devices around identity and intent in order to deceive. It is the experience of being deceived, being strung along, that not simply galls but shapes the self-perception of the victim. Unlike the burgled householder or mugged shopper, the fraud victim has participated in a relationship that has turned into a cruel or uncomfortable hoax. It is the abuse of trust and its negative consequences for social status and self respect that appears prominent in these and other fraud cases against private citizens, and which seems to mark them out as different to other crime victims. Other victims of ordinary street crime can draw some comfort from the belief that their injury was somehow random, that they did not intend to place themselves in jeopardy or engage in some relationship that would lead them to being robbed or physically injured (though victim self-blame can occur, as in family violence, in many areas of supposed 'victim-precipitation'). This sense of status injury would seem to lend itself to a determination to 'do something' to remedy events. Hence, the term 'victim' in the context of these respondents suggests a dynamic status that shifts in a process of self-ascription and subsequent action. That is, the individual victims apply their own appraisal (and re-appraisal) of the unintended part they played in the fraud and they orient their conduct towards the crime and fraudster accordingly. It is this process, particularly in respect of known local fraudsters, that provides the opportunity for some victims to believe in their own capacity to challenge events.

These victims of fraud could not be described as having lost all confidence in their capacity to judge risks and avoid victimisation in the future. Nonetheless, they intimated some damage to their own sense of self esteem and their willingness to trust others in conditions of uncertainty similar to those surrounding the case in question. It is this realm of the uncertain in our social encounters that is so susceptible to the 'methodology' of fraud, and it through a phenomenological methodology of the everyday world and allied quantitative methods that fraud, as symbolic construction and as a social harm, is best explained.

References

Bok, S. (1978) *Lying: Moral Choice in Public and Private Life,* Pantheon, New York.
Becker, E. (1972) *The Birth and Death of Meaning,* Penguin, Harmondsworth.
Cicourel, A. (1964) *Method and Measurement in Sociology,* Free Press, New York.
Dasgupta, P. (1988) 'Trust as a commodity', in D. Gambetta (ed) *Trust: Making and Breaking Co-operative Relations,* Blackwell, Oxford.
Denzin, N., (1970) *Sociological Methods: A Source Book,* Butterworths, London.
Eisenstadt, S. and Roniger, L. (1984) *Patrons, Clients and Friends: Interpersonal Relations and the Structure of Trust in Society,* Cambridge University Press, Cambridge.
Fukuyama, F. (1995) *Trust,* Hamish Hamilton, London.

Garfinkel, H. (1967) *Studies in Ethnomethodology,* Prentice-Hall, New Jersey.

Goffman, E. (1971) *The Presentation of Self in Everyday Life,* Pelican, Harmondsworth.

Good, D. (1988) Individuals, interpersonal relations, and trust, in Gambetta, D. (ed) *Trust: Making and Breaking in Co-operative Relations,* Blackwell, Oxford.

Hammersley, M. and Atkinson, P. (1995) *Ethnography: Principles into Practice,* Routledge, London.

Holstein, J. Gubrium, A. and Jaber, F. (1995) *The Active Interview,* Sage, Beverly Hills.

Jones, R. (1996) *Research Methods in the Social and Behavioural Sciences,* Sinauer Associates, Mass.

Levi, M. and Pithouse, A. (1999) *Victims of Fraud: The Social and Media Construction of White Collar Crime,* Oxford University Press, Oxford, (forthcoming).

McCracken, G. (1988) *The Long Interview,* Sage, Beverly Hills.

Miller, G. and Dingwall, R. (eds.) (1997) *Context and Method in Qualitative Research,* Sage, London.

Punch, M. (1996) *Dirty Business: Exploring Corporate Misconduct,* Sage, London.

Rutter, J. (1980) Interpersonal trust, trustworthiness, and gullibility, *American Psychologist,* 35, pp. 1-7.

Titus, R., Heinzelmann, F. and Boyle, J. (1995) 'Victimization of persons by fraud', *Crime & Delinquency,* 41, pp. 54-72.

Walsh, M. and Schram, D. (1980) 'The victim of white-collar crime: accuser or accused?', in Stotland, E. and Geis, G. (eds) *White-Collar Crime: Theory and Research,* Sage, Beverly Hills.